RANCH GIRL

RANCH GIRL

COMING OF AGE ON THE KING RANCHES IN BRAZIL

BETINHA SCHULTZ *and* JACK SCHULTZ

FORT WORTH, TEXAS

LIBRARY OF CONGRESS CATALOGING-IN-PUBLICATION DATA

Names: Schultz, Betinha, author. | Schultz, Jack, 1952– author. | Hanlon, Thomas W., author.

Title: Ranch girl : coming of age on the King ranches in Brazil / Betinha Schultz and Jack Schultz, with Tom Hanlon.

Description: Fort Worth : TCU Press, [2023] | Summary: "At nine months of age, Betinha Emmert Schultz moved with her parents from New Mexico to rural Brazil, where she spent the next 14 years of her life. From her earliest memories to those of a teenager about to be sent off to boarding school, Betinha recounts the challenges and trials, the richness and beauty, and the sometimes hard but always good life lessons she learned while growing up as the daughter of the manager of multiple King Ranches in Brazil" — Provided by publisher.

Identifiers: LCCN 2022047225 (print) | LCCN 2022047226 (ebook) | ISBN 9780875658384 (cloth) | ISBN 9780875658438 (ebook)

Subjects: LCSH: Schultz, Betinha. | Schultz, Betinha—Childhood and youth. | Schultz, Betinha—Family. | Schultz, Betinha—Homes and haunts—Brazil—Mato Grosso (State) | King Ranch, Inc.—History. | Girls—Brazil—Mato Grosso (State)—Biography. | Americans—Brazil—Mato Grosso (State)—Biography. | Ranchers—Brazil—Mato Grosso (State)—Biography. | Ranch life—Brazil—Mato Grosso (State) | Ranch life—Texas—History. | Mato Grosso (Brazil : State)—Social life and customs. | LCGFT: Autobiographies.

Classification: LCC F2659.A5 S38 2023 (print) | LCC F2659.A5 (ebook) |

TCU Box 298300
Fort Worth, Texas 76129

Design by Julie Rushing

We dedicate this book to our beautiful granddaughters, Sophie and Ava. May your life be filled with all of the wonder and excitement that B experienced.

CONTENTS

ACKNOWLEDGMENTS

Ranch Girl: Coming of Age on the King Ranches in Brazil would not have been possible without the support of several people. A special thank you to our writer Tom Hanlon. Tom is simply amazing and beautifully articulated our ideas and stories into a final product that we are so very proud of.

This book project was pushed to the finish line by Sarah Horner. Sarah has "quarterbacked" many projects for me over the years, and we are grateful that she saw how special this one was to our family and ran with this one as well. Thank you, Sarah, for coordinating everything and keeping us on track!

To Janet Grunloh and Lisa Huston, thank you for assisting with editing, scanning pictures, and all the other tasks associated with making *Ranch Girl* a reality.

Our sons, James and Joseph, their wives, and our two precious granddaughters are the ones who inspired us to put this wonderful part of their history on paper. May you cherish it as much we enjoyed putting it together for you.

CHAPTER 1

BORN TO BE A COWBOY

MY FATHER, PETE EMMERT, was born in Corpus Christi, Texas, in 1931, while his father, Buck, was off playing polo in Mexico.

That might, at a glance, seem harsh, especially in today's world, where many fathers are present for the birth of their children. But that was not the way of the world back in the 1930s, and it definitely was not the way of Buck. Were Buck alive today, it almost certainly would *still* not be his way.

Buck was a ranch manager in South Texas, and was in Mexico because Jonas Weil, the ranch owner, sent him there to show off the ranch's mustangs. Weil and many other Texas ranchers believed that mustangs were ideal for polo. Buck was a good rider. So Buck accompanied a team to Mexico to show off the ponies in action.

Duty called, and Buck responded. Besides, he was a man's man, well-suited to running a ranch with twenty or so ranch hands under him. To be around a woman giving birth would neither have appeal nor make any sense to him; what could he do? Deliver the baby himself? A calf, sure. A foal, of course.

Like most men in the 1930s and '40s, he adhered to a strong division of labor in the household, with his work being confined to the outdoors, the running of the ranch, and his wife's duties covering the childbirthing, the cleaning, cooking, the laundering, and most certainly the changing of diapers. That clearly was women's work.

Welcome to the world of my grandfather, Albert "Buck" Emmert.

No one dared call him "Albert," and his grandkids never called him "Grandpa," "Grandfather," or anything else other than "Buck."

When Buck returned from his Mexican trip, he found his wife, Mabel, sitting in the front room of their house on the ranch that Buck managed. The window offered a sweeping view of the semi-arid land, which was covered with mesquite.

"Heard you had a boy," he said. Buck was nothing if not straightforward. He spoke in a very distinct style, the result of suffering for years in his youth as a stutterer, a problem that was overcome only after he was sent to a special school in the Midwest. For the rest of his life, Buck spoke slowly and rhythmically, carefully choosing his words and, more to the point, his pronunciation of them. You could see him think through everything he said. Combined with his abrupt, no-nonsense manner and deep, rather monotone voice, everything that he said carried a heavier weight, a gravitas, than most people's words. You can believe his ranch hands hung on his every word, and then set to carrying them out. But then, so did everyone else he spoke to.

"He's beautiful," Mabel smiled. "I named him Albert Emanuel Emmert."

"Why on earth would you do that?" Buck groused. Mabel was a sweet and soft-spoken woman who regularly incurred the wrath of her husband. I will say this about Buck, however: he rarely if ever raised his voice or flew off the handle. He didn't need to. The look on his stern face, the unyielding glare, the tone of voice, and the rumble of judgment, disdain, and dissatisfaction—like the booming of distant thunder headed your way—was enough to get his point across with absolute authority.

"Well, because they're family names," Mabel said. "They're his grandfathers' names. And *yours.*" This neither moved nor appeased Buck. He just stared at her as if she were crazy, or a little soft in the head. Buck was not mean to Mabel, but he did not—likely could not—show affection. He and Mabel didn't even eat together; Buck ate at the camp house with the ranch hands. Later, when Mabel had a stroke, he sent her off to be taken care of by two of their daughters in the Rio Grande Valley, while he stayed in the house outside of Refugio he had bought upon retiring. Buck, ever frugal, figured their daughters could provide the care Mabel needed as well as a nursing home, and for a lot less money. Again, this was not being mean to Mabel; it was taking care of her in the way he knew how. Still, Mabel's sisters always felt sorry for her, isolated on the ranch with Buck.

Buck snorted. "Let me see him."

"He's sleeping in his crib. We shouldn't disturb him."

"Get him."

Mabel got up and went into the bedroom laid out for the baby and rousted my father from his sleep, but he drowsed off again on the way out to the front room. Buck peered into the infant's face for several moments, then nodded. He had come to a decision.

"I'm calling him Pete. He looks like a Pete to me."

"'Pete'? But what about 'Albert'?"

He gave her an unequivocal look. "He's Pete."

Just as no one called Buck by his given name, no one would ever call my father, Albert Emanuel Emmert, by his given name. What was good enough for Buck was good enough for Pete.

Some people are born with an open map in front of them; they can choose which way they want to go, what they want to do with their lives. Others enter this world with their route seemingly already mapped out for them. They couldn't veer from their path if they tried.

My dad, Albert Emanuel (Pete) Emmert, was solidly in this latter group.

Buck raised Pete to be like he was: a man's man. Pete was Buck's oldest child, and, as it turned out, his only son (Pete had four sisters, all of whom rode in rodeos, as did Pete: Mary Jo, Pat, Margaret, and Ann). Pete learned to crawl, then walk, then work. He had a problem relaxing his whole life; he always had to be doing something, preferably outdoors, with his hands.

"Texas wasn't built by slackers sitting inside drinking a cup of tea," I could imagine Buck telling my dad before Pete even set foot inside a schoolhouse. "It was built on the backs of men who weren't afraid to sweat, who worked hard to get done what needed to get done. You understand?"

I could see my dad solemnly nodding. Yes, of course he understood.

And he showed he did by working hard, doing what needed to be done. There was never-ending work to be done, and none of it half-heartedly. Pete took to his work with a gusto, partly because he liked being outdoors and working with the cattle and horses, and partly because he wanted to live up to Buck's very high expectations—which, amazingly, he did. As hard as Buck was, he acknowledged that Pete was a good worker, though he rarely let his son know that firsthand. Buck was of the "spare the rod, spoil the child" ilk; a compliment from Buck was a rarity indeed, occurring only slightly more regularly than Halley's comet, which appears every seventy-six years. He wasn't one to spoil his kids with presents, either: for Christmas, Pete generally got a shirt, and he better like it. And not get it dirty working with the steers on Christmas afternoon.

Understand that Buck worked from sunup to sundown, and he expected everyone on the ranch to do likewise. Pete always kept a hammer handy, and if he saw Buck walking up, he would start hammering as if he were fixing something.

Early on, Pete began to raise steers, showing them in 4-H fairs from middle school through high school. From 1946 through 1949 he was a four-time Nueces County Junior Livestock Champion Exhibitor, with three grand champions and one reserve grand champion in the steer competitions. He also trained horses and always rode a horse that he was breaking to his all-boys Catholic high school west of Corpus Christi. "It beat walking by a long shot," he would tell me later. He would work with the horse on the way to the school, which adjoined the ranch, stall it in a cousin's nearby pen, and resume its training at the end of the school day.

He used horses for other purposes, too. I learned that while he was either a senior in high school or a freshman in college, he found occasion to ride in the summer to the neighboring ranch where he would clandestinely meet with his own version of Mrs. Robinson (from the movie *The Graduate*), a married woman who introduced Pete to the art of lovemaking. Had Buck ever found this out, Pete might not have made it through his college years, but the fact that he lost his virginity to his married neighbor mercifully was found out by neither the cuckolded husband nor by Buck.

During his later high school years Pete spent his summers on a ranch in Hebbronville, about four hours south of Refugio, where he lived on the other ranch that was owned by Jonas Weil. He went so he could earn some money for college—and, while he of course didn't mention this to Buck, so he could get away from him and have a little fun, which was a rare commodity at home. Buck saw no need for humor or fun on a ranch; it would slow down the work and entirely miss the point of ranching. If you want to have *fun*, go waste your time indoors at a desk job. If you weren't man enough to work outdoors, that is.

Pete had a lot of Buck in him, but he also had some of the liveliness and restlessness of the typical young man, someone who was looking for a bit of adventure and, dammit all, *fun*. So he and some of his buddies would hook on at the ranch in Hebbronville, just north of the Mexican border, and they would work hard during the day and play hard at night, frequenting the local watering holes and bantering with (and sometimes doing more with) the *señoritas bonitas*, the pretty young ladies, who looked mighty good to the young men. Young men who looked pretty good themselves, with their work-hardened muscles and their sun-bronzed bodies. Pete would often rely on beer to replenish the fluid he had sweated out during the day, and the beer could fuel both romantic evenings with the *señoritas* and fun-filled nights highlighted by pranks, such as driving about an hour south of Hebbronville to cross into Mexico—no border guards either way those days—and transport outhouses from fields to the town square in Nueva Ciudad Guerrero, just across the Rio Grande.

Even with his fun-loving side, Pete was never derelict in his duties. He could always be counted on to do his work and then some, and to do it well. That part of him was inbred, drilled into him from the time he could walk.

And he had another reason for working hard: he was earning money to pay for his college. Buck was all for Pete going to college; he simply wasn't going to pay for any of it (even though he put all four of his daughters through college). So Pete worked hard in the summers to save for college, and when he was in college—he attended what was then Texas A&I and is now Texas A&M University in Kingsville, about an hour south of Refugio—he worked the rodeo circuit in the summers, riding bulls and broncos to pay for his tuition and room and board, with maybe a few beers thrown in just to keep him hydrated.

Buck's idea of fun was to accomplish a work task. Short of that, he would make saddles and hackamores—bridles without bits—in his workshop. He occasionally read, too—he'd thumb through the dictionary, or read about combustion engines. Enthralling stuff. Then he'd talk to his grandkids about words he'd come across, or how the fuel in a combustion engine mixes with air and ignites, causing combustion. We would try to appear interested. (In general, though, even if we didn't find his talks about combustion engines to be very captivating, we found *him* both fascinating and endearing, as only the grandchildren of a very gruff and unusual man could.)

Pete's idea of fun, on the other hand, was transporting outhouses to Mexican town squares, or becoming the paramour of an older woman, or riding on a bull or bronco while drunk. Which he did often enough on the summer circuits that started in Texas and took him to New Mexico, Arizona, Colorado, Wyoming, and beyond. It was like keeping a greyhound pent up in a kennel for nine months before someone mercifully opened his cage and let him roam the countryside. Pete had perhaps an extra dose of youthful exuberance, an exaggerated wild streak, because of Buck's heavy-handed, no-nonsense way of life. Once Pete broke free of that short chain on the ranch at home, anything was fair game. He and a few of his college buddies would pile into his old Chevy that was big enough to haul saddles, other rodeo gear, and cowboys, heading for the next rodeo on the map with a few pitstops in between for burgers and beer. On one of those trips he knocked out a friend's tooth over a disagreement that neither of them could remember the next day.

Buck, of course, knew none of this beyond that his son was going off to rodeos to earn money for college. He begrudgingly let Pete go ride the broncs and bulls at rodeos because he sure wasn't going to pay his son's tuition.

Pete spent two years at Texas A&I before he and four of his pals decided to enlist in the Air Force in 1951 to serve during the Korean War. His reasoning was simple: the rodeos were not going to earn him enough money to go through school, but the GI Bill would. He chose the Air Force because he figured he would see less action. As it turned out, his four friends were all rejected, primarily for vision issues, but Pete's vision was fine—he never needed glasses or contacts his whole life—so he enlisted and was stationed at Chanute Air Force Base in Rantoul, Illinois. Rantoul was like a foreign country to a young Texan—instead of thousands of acres of ranch land, dotted with steers and horses, he was surrounded by thousands of acres of soybean and corn fields, and he rarely saw cowboy boots or hats on anyone. Even though Rantoul was a town of only about six thousand at the time, it had a citified feel to it, compared to Texas. About the only thing he could relate to home was the military approach to life. Buck had certainly prepared him for that.

Pete was discharged from the Air Force in January of 1955 and returned to Texas A&I on the GI Bill. He roomed on campus with Bud

Bonner, who was dating Mary Lee Green at the time. Bud and Mary Lee went on a few double dates with Pete and one of Mary Lee's friends, and Mary Lee soon found her attention was stolen by this good-looking veteran who had been to Hong Kong, Japan, and other locales when he had been stationed in Taiwan.

Mary Lee never had a problem in going after what she wanted. And what she wanted was Pete. So one late spring afternoon in Kingsville, she made a date with Pete in a coffee shop on campus. She wore a low-cut red dress with small white polka dots and thin shoulder straps. Her perfume, Chanel No. 5, gave off a fresh, flowery scent, which found its way into Pete's nostrils as he sat across from her at a small table. He had a Coke while she had a coffee.

"So tell me what it was like in the Air Force," Mary Lee said.

"It was mainly boring. Have you ever been to Rantoul, Illinois?"

Mary Lee took a sip of her coffee. Pete was having a hard time pretending not to notice how much soft skin the dress revealed around her shoulders and near her cleavage.

"No, but you went overseas, right? That's what you mentioned the other night."

Pete nodded and Mary Lee listened, enraptured, as he told about being stationed in Taiwan. He told her of the beauty of Taipei, two hours to the north of the air base; Taipei is bordered by rivers on the south and west and has a beautiful view of Qixing Mountain and Mt. Datun to the north, in addition to a nearby national park. To the south of the city are the Songshan Hills and the Qingshui Cliffs, which form a dense and rich woods.

"That sounds gorgeous," Mary Lee said.

"It was a little different from dusty, dry Texas, that's for sure."

"So, tell me more."

Pete told her about his trips to Hong Kong and Japan, about eating the various delicacies and barbecued pork, which didn't taste at all like Texas barbecue, about the steamed shrimp dumplings and sushi and miso soup, about going to horse races in Hong Kong and hiking through the Arashiyama Bamboo Forest near Kyoto in Japan, and white water rafting down the Tone River near Minakami.

"Bud tells me you're into rodeos, too?" Mary Lee said.

"Yep. Besides Texas, I've been to rodeos in New Mexico and Arizona. I plan to go to the Cheyenne rodeo this summer and some more up in that area. It's a good way to make money."

"Wow, you really travel a lot," Mary Lee said.

"I like to get out." He mentioned trips to the Grand Canyon, Big Bend National Park, and Pedernales Falls State Park. "I guess I have been around," he said, perhaps a bit too casually, as he was trying to impress Mary Lee. "You like horse races?"

"I don't know, I've never been to one."

"Well, you're missing something. One of my favorite things to do is go to the horse races in Reynosa."

"Mexico? You do get around, don't you?"

Pete shrugged, grinning. "Better than staying at home, I guess."

Mary Lee was from Sinton, a town of about 4,200 back then, but she always thought of herself as possessing the charm and sophistication

Pete Emmert, Grand Canyon, 1952. Author collection.

befitting a lady from Dallas or San Antonio. Even so, she was impressed with Pete. Which meant that Bud Bonner, who was to become a lifelong friend of Pete's, saw his best friend start to date—and get serious with—the girl who was once his.

During the summer break, she told her father, Bill Green, her Aunt Ruby, and Mrs. Landrum, Aunt Ruby's friend, all about Pete. (Mary Lee's mother passed away when Mary Lee was a teenager, and Mrs. Landrum helped Bill look after her.)

"I'm dating the best-looking cowboy you've ever seen!" Mary Lee told them one early summer evening, her face flushed with excitement. They were on Bill's front porch, drinking lemonade.

Bill was a kind man and loved his daughter greatly, but he couldn't quite hide his smirk.

"What are you grinning at?" Mary Lee demanded.

"Nothing, sweetheart. It's just that . . . well, it's hard to picture you with a 'cowboy.'"

"I always envisioned you in Dallas, or maybe even Los Angeles or New York," Aunt Ruby chimed in.

"Well now, I imagine Mary Lee can do whatever she sets her mind to, and that includes dating cowboys," said Mrs. Landrum.

"I'm glad that *someone* believes in me," Mary Lee said.

"I agree, Mrs. Landrum," Bill said. "And it's not like she's going to *marry* this feller . . . " he turned to Mary Lee. "Are you?"

She stuck her nose up in the air. "I just might."

Bill stared at his daughter for a moment, shocked. He knew college sometimes put crazy notions in young people's heads, but not *this* crazy.

"I'm sorry," he said, "but I'm having a hard time seeing you living in the country, darling."

That was enough for Mary Lee. She stomped off, furious, wishing she could turn around again and go see Pete. And besides, even if they were right about her living in the country, she didn't *plan* to live in the country. She was no country bumpkin. She planned on living in a city, preferably a *big* city, where she and Pete could have one adventure after another. She'd had enough of the dirt and dust of South Texas. She knew she could talk Pete into anything.

That fall, back in school, Pete popped the question (ironically, they were parked near the front gate of the King Ranch at the time). Mary Lee hugged and kissed him and said, "It's about time!"

When Pete introduced Mary Lee to his parents, Buck and Mary Lee got off on the wrong foot, and they pretty much stayed that way until Buck was buried.

"Where you from?" Buck asked Mary Lee upon first meeting her at the ranch. Buck and Mabel were sitting in chairs in the living room, facing Mary Lee and Pete, who were on a couch.

"Sinton. That okay with you?" Mary Lee shot back. She was in a foul mood for some reason, and even in her good moods, she didn't take guff off of people.

Buck raised an eyebrow at her. "I see we got a sassy one here."

Mabel said nothing, because she never contradicted Buck, but it was clear she liked Mary Lee.

"I don't see anything wrong with being sassy," Mary Lee said. "Do you?"

"Are you Catholic?" Buck asked in that odd rhythmic speaking style of his, ignoring her question.

"No. I was raised Methodist, but then most of my friends were Baptist, so I switched over," Mary Lee said.

"You switched," Buck said.

"Yes. I switched. Didn't I already say that?"

Buck sat up a little straighter in his chair. Pete watched his dad's eyes; he could see the spark in them again. He also thought he caught the slightest hint of a grin on his face—a rare occurrence. Maybe Buck was thinking, *This one here's a live wire. Could be interesting.*

"Usually people switch when they don't have no strong convictions of their own," Buck said.

"Well, Mr. Emmert, I can tell you this. I have plenty of strong convictions, and I'm happy to share them with you."

Buck just watched her for a bit and then nodded. He apparently liked that answer. "Well," he said, looking at Mabel and then at Pete before back at Mary Lee, "I'll tell you one thing. You want to marry Pete, the only way you're doing that is in a Catholic church. So you got to switch religions. Again."

Mary Lee stared right back at Buck. She let a little time pass for dramatic effect.

"And I'll tell you two things, Buck Emmert. I'm fine with changing to Catholicism. That's no big thing to me. You know why? Because I'm not switching *religions.* It's all Christian, if I'm not mistaken."

Buck looked over at Mabel. "I'll be damned," he said. "She called me 'Buck.'"

Mabel just gave a little Mona Lisa smile. She must have been enjoying the sass that this girl was spraying at Buck.

"No girl called me by my first name before."

"Look, *Mr. Emmert,* I love your son. I plan to marry him. I have no problems becoming a Catholic. And you know what? I have no problems if you don't like me that much. Because I'm not marrying you. I'm marrying *him.*" She pointed at Pete, who was half astonished and half giddy at how Mary Lee was standing up to Buck.

"Good on ya," Buck said in a way that everyone understood was the final word on the subject. "Go make yourself a Catholic. Go marry this guy. And keep calling me Buck. I don't mind."

Both Pete's and Mabel's jaws dropped at that. But for the moment, at least, there was peace between Buck and Mary Lee.

They were married over Thanksgiving weekend in 1956 in the Catholic church in Sinton. The ceremony did not pass, of course, without its share of mini-dramas. For one, because Mary Lee had not yet been baptized as a Catholic, they could not get married at the regular altar, so they spoke their vows at a makeshift altar halfway down the aisle. Mary Lee, who was not thrilled with the protocol to begin with, neither forgot nor forgave the church for this perceived slight.

During the ceremony, which was a small gathering with family and a few friends, one of Pete's sisters sobbed the whole way through. His other sisters didn't cry, but all were upset that Pete was marrying Mary Lee, who didn't seem to fit into the Emmert ideal for a rancher's wife (and indeed, Mary Lee at the time had no plans to be a rancher's wife; just as she had been converted to Catholicism, she had her sights set on converting Pete to a life lived in more "civilized" circumstances).

Mary Lee's side of the family was horrified that she was converting from Protestantism to Catholicism, getting married in a Catholic church, and being slapped in the face by not being allowed to be married at the regular altar.

Pretty much everyone at the wedding was annoyed, angry, or upset for one reason or another—including Buck, who was aghast when he saw Pete enter the church in *dress shoes.*

"What are those you got on your feet?" he asked in the back of the church.

Pete looked down at his shoes, which were pinching his toes. Neither he nor Buck had ever worn dress shoes in their lives. But Mary Lee insisted, saying she was not going to marry "some cowboy in boots with dung all over them."

When Pete mentioned this to his father, Buck said, "Well, you have a nice pair of black boots. You could have worn those."

"Not if I want to get through this wedding alive," Pete said.

Buck just shook his head. What had his son gotten himself into?

My father, Albert Emanuel (Pete) Emmert, may have gotten married in dress shoes. But he was more like Buck than sometimes he'd like to admit, because I'm sure he would have preferred to wear boots to his wedding.

Mary Lee Green might have squelched the cowboy in him on their wedding day, at least a bit. But there was no way she was going to convert him from cowboy to city slicker or anything else.

Pete Emmert was born to be a cowboy, born to manage a ranch. In that way, he was following in both his father's and his grandfather's footsteps.

And those steps were taken in bona fide cowboy boots. Sturdy, dirty, worn, comfortable boots, made for working.

CHAPTER 2

"LIFE IS LIKE BULL WRANGLING"

MY PARENTS HONEYMOONED IN REYNOSA, MEXICO, which is on the southern bank of the Rio Grande. While it was literally a stone's throw from McAllen, Texas, it *was* an international honeymoon, and that held a certain allure for my mother. They stayed at a resort, went to the horse races in the afternoons, danced in the evenings, and had a few discussions about what to do with the generous gift of one hundred dollars from Pete's future employer, John Tatton. (That amount is worth about nine hundred dollars now.) Mary Lee, never having come across a dollar she didn't mind spending, wanted to spend the entire sum on their honeymoon—more specifically, on the ponies. Pete, a bit (okay, *way*) more grounded financially than Mary Lee, thought it wise to save some of that money.

Shockingly, Mary Lee lost this argument. They did go to a few horse races, and plunked down some of those dollars, but they saved most of the money. It was one of the few arguments I ever knew of her losing.

After their honeymoon, they returned to Kingsville, Texas, so Pete could finish his senior year of college. They rented an upstairs apartment in a house and quickly made friends with other young couples in the neighborhood. As spring arrived, they started throwing block parties with their friends, barbecuing chicken, ribs, and burgers, cranking up someone's transistor radio to listen to Elvis ("Don't Be Cruel," "Heartbreak Hotel," "Blue Suede Shoes"), Little Richard ("Good

Golly Miss Molly," "Lucille"), and Buddy Holly ("Peggy Sue," "That'll Be the Day"), and wetting their whistles with Lone Stars and PBRs. During one of these festive bashes, a young man selling encyclopedias showed up in a sweat-stained shirt, his sleeves rolled up, hauling a cartful of encyclopedias behind him. Probably more because he was tired and thirsty, rather than in hot pursuit of a sale, he dropped his cart handle to the ground, wiped his brow with a handkerchief, and nodded hello to Pete, who promptly grabbed him a cold Lone Star from a cooler.

"You look like you could use a drink," Pete said.

"It is hot," the salesman agreed before taking a long, cool drink.

"Watcha got there?" Pete said, nodding toward the cart.

"Encyclopedias. Gateway to the world," the young man said. He took another long drink. "Man, this hits the spot."

The party had been in full swing for a while, and most of the folks there had amply wet their whistles and were quite happy to have a newcomer join them. They crowded around the young man, who by this time was on his second beer, and they good-naturedly started quizzing him on subject matter.

"What's the life expectancy of a raccoon?" one asked.

"About thirty seconds if I got my .22 handy," another drolly said.

"Who invented the Slinky?" someone else asked.

"Well, uh . . . " the salesman said.

"Better yet, *why* did he invent the Slinky? Does it really contribute a lot to mankind?"

They all let him know they were just kidding him, and someone handed him another beer, which he gratefully drank down as the tinny music blared to the best of its ability from the radio.

"How much you selling those for?" Pete asked.

"These?" the young man said, pointing to his books. "Well, these are *Encyclopedia Britannica*s, you know. Top of the line. First came into print around 1770. Nearly half a million topics, almost 40 million words in just one set."

Someone whistled. "You read all those words?"

He grinned but ignored the question, instead returning to Pete's query about the price. He gave Pete a quote.

"Those'd come in handy," he said. "But they're a bit pricey."

Soon the salesman had a third beer handed to him, and soon that beer was consumed.

And right after that, the salesman offered them a cut-rate deal, the terms of which were delivered in a hushed tone, as if he feared the encyclopedia publishers were nearby.

The salesman wrote up multiple orders that day. Whether he sold my parents and their friends, or they sold him, is hard to say. But my parents bought the books, and later bought a special mahogany case for them, and both the encyclopedias and the case were in the family until 2018, when my sister sold them to a home-schooling family. (We lugged the *Britannica*s all the way to Brazil with us, and our friends used to rip pages out of the last book to roll joints: the paper was ideal for it, they claimed. "Besides, who's ever going to look in the Zs?")

When they weren't sitting around reading their encyclopedias, Pete was working on finishing his degree in agriculture at Texas A&I (now Texas A&M)-Kingsville, while Mary Lee was teaching English at a public high school in Kingsville. The schools back then were segregated in Texas, and the school she taught at was Hispanic. It was a rough school in a tough, working-class neighborhood. The students were frisked for knives every morning they came into the school.

She loved in later years to lord it over Pete that she had "put him through school"—even if that only meant that she had been the breadwinner during his final semester. She also told me, many years later, that back then a woman had three choices: be a secretary, a nurse, or a teacher. She wasn't cut out to take orders from somebody as a secretary, and to be a nurse, she said, "You had to deal with male genitalia," and she wasn't about to do that.

So, she became a teacher, at least for a bit.

She also let Pete know in addition to the great sacrifice of "putting him through school" that she was making, she was also putting her very life out on a limb for him every day, just by showing up at her school.

At times, Pete would roll his eyes and say "Oh come on, Mary Lee. Is it really *that* bad?"

Which of course was the wrong thing to say, because then he would spend the next half hour getting an earful of just how bad it really was—not to mention how easy it was for him, being merely a student.

But things would soon go from bad to worse in Mary Lee's eyes.

Pete graduated in May of 1957. But while he had spent his last semester student teaching, he really had no illusions of setting foot in a classroom once he graduated. He more or less undertook student teaching to establish once and for all what he knew back when he was a kid: he was born to work outdoors.

John Tatton, who also owned the Salt Creek Ranch in Refugio that Buck worked on, hired Pete to run the Canon del Agua Ranch that he owned near Las Vegas. No, not the one with the neon lights, gambling, shopping, entertainment, and night life (all of which would have suited Mary Lee just fine). This was Las Vegas, *New Mexico*, which is about seven hundred miles from Las Vegas, *Nevada*, but is about a million miles away in terms of living conditions. Las Vegas, New Mexico, is about an hour east of Santa Fe, but Mary Lee would more likely have geographically described it as "The Armpit of Hell."

The ranch, of course, was outside of Las Vegas, about an hour west of the town, in the Santa Fe Mountains, a subrange of the Sangre de Cristo ("Blood of Christ") Mountains. The mountains surround the Pecos Wilderness, a protected wilderness area, and includes Truchas Peak, a 13,102-foot mountain in which the upper desert ranch was nestled. Canon del Agua was a cow-calf operation—that is, it was a beef cattle operation in which a permanent herd of cows was kept to produce calves for later sale. The ranch was remote, cold, desolate, with a vista of wide-open spaces and a treacherous two-lane road that at times in the winter was made impassable by the snows and howling winds that would blow off the mountains.

Pete went out to the ranch as Mary Lee was wrapping up her teaching duties. Buck and Mabel later drove Mary Lee to the ranch, and she cried the whole way; she knew what she was getting into. This was definitely *not* what she had in mind when she married Pete. A ranch in Texas she could put up with; a ranch in New Mexico, plopped on some mountain that made Siberia seem cheery by comparison, with just a couple of cowboys living in a bunkhouse and a foreman with a family to talk to, was a bit much.

Especially when she was pregnant.

Which she was, with me.

She had found that out shortly before Buck and Mabel drove her to New Mexico. She didn't tell them at the time; she hadn't even told Pete yet. But it surely added to the bitterness of her tears on the ride to the ranch; she was no doubt mortified that her firstborn was destined to be born in New Mexico rather than Texas. (It was well understood in Mary Lee's world that all good Texans, if at all possible, return to the Lone Star State to give birth—in part because Texans don't consider someone a real Texan unless they are born there.) Even her teaching job in Kingsville, where, to paraphrase the old hockey saying, she went to a fight and a class broke out, was better than this. Mary Lee, understand, was a social person; she needed people around her like flowers need sun and water. Preferably people who could fawn over her and make her feel like the queen she saw herself as, or perhaps people she could boss around and explain how to do things correctly; but at its base level, she needed people around her. Not coyotes, elk, antelope, and bobcats.

She was also, to be honest, very self-centered. The world was made to orbit around her, cater to her whims. She was a cheerleader in high school, and she refused to go see her mother, who was dying in a hospital, because she was in the midst of cheerleading trials. By the time the trials were over, her mother had passed away. Yet when I asked her once if she ever felt guilty about that, she replied "Why should I? My mother had been on the verge of dying before. How was I supposed to know she would really die that day?"

It's tough, you see, for a self-centered person to live in isolation. Self-centeredness only stands out in juxtaposition to the importance you attach to others in your life. How can you be self-centered when no one is around for you to ignore?

"What are you sniffling for?" Buck said as they neared Canon del Agua.

"Why did he have to take this job?" Mary Lee said. "Could this *be* more desolate?"

Buck no doubt couldn't understand my mother's thinking. He never could. To him, a job was a job, and you should be damn glad to have one; John Tatton was a good man and worth working for. Pete should consider himself lucky to land a ranch manager's job fresh out of college, and it was not a lifelong commitment, anyway. The unspoken but generally understood plan was for Pete to take over the Salt Creek Ranch back in Refugio once Buck retired. And that wasn't that far down the road.

And wasn't a wife supposed to support her husband in his career? Pete had jokingly told him about Mary Lee bragging about putting him through college at the end of his academic days; well, now she could settle into her duties as a ranch manager's wife, let him support her, and get on with life. With a little less complaining, ideally.

Buck was likely thinking all this, but he and my mother had tussled enough over the past few years that he knew when to push back and when not to. He had, after all, broken plenty of horses in his day.

So he just said "You'll be all right. Just give it a chance." To which my mother doubtless muttered something underneath her breath.

The main house at the Canon del Agua Ranch was a nice enough place. But when Pete greeted her with open arms and a big smile, saying "Welcome home!" she burst into tears and found a bedroom to cry in. Buck, in the living room with his son, just shrugged and said "Good luck," and he and Mabel left the newlyweds to their new life.

My mother once told me that life is like bull wrangling. The bull runs out of the chute, and to wrangle it, you have to time your jump just right. If you're too slow or too fast, you lose your chance. The bull beats you.

To beat the bull, you have to grab your opportunity at the exact right moment. You can't hesitate or doubt yourself. You just jump on the damn bull and wrangle it to the ground.

That's how she lived her life.

A month or two before I was due, my parents rented an apartment in Las Vegas. There was no way my mother was going to stay at the ranch, in the mountains, with the treacherous winter roads, and risk having a home birth (I was born in late February of 1958). My dad completely understood and agreed, and they got a little place in town, and I was born at the Catholic hospital in Las Vegas.

My mother was relieved to be in town, but she was not happy that she had to go to a Catholic hospital. Her experience with the Catholic Church, understand, was limited to being humiliated by exchanging their wedding vows halfway up the aisle, because she was not Catholic and not deemed good enough to go all the way up the aisle. So she had a boulder-sized chip on her shoulder about the Catholic Church, one that she carried throughout her life. And one that, at least, was made heavier by the poor treatment she claimed she got from the nuns in the hospital. She told me later that they were mean to her; they didn't give her enough pain meds, and so on.

The thing about Mary Lee Emmert is this: she either liked you or she didn't. And she wasn't shy about letting you know if it was the latter.

And so I began my life on a snowy mountain in desolate New Mexico. And, being Pete Emmert's daughter, of course I have a picture of him holding me on a horse before I was able to walk or talk. In the Emmert family, that seemed to be the natural progression of skills. While most infants were being swaddled and cuddled and dressed in cute outfits, I was being plopped on a horse by my father.

It was never too early, in his mind, to learn about horses.

When my mother didn't like a situation, she didn't sit passively by. She would grab the bull by the horns, twist, and bring it down. And the situation would change; she would wrangle it to her own satisfaction.

So, when she came across an ad in *Cattleman's Quarterly* for ranch manager jobs in Brazil, the wheels in her head began swiftly turning. Brazil! A foreign country. With much more intrigue—and better weather—than what she likely saw as her prison term on the Canon del Agua Ranch. She did a little research in the encyclopedias they had bought: Brazil has almost 60 percent of the Amazon Rainforest. It has reputedly the best coffee in the world. And monkeys galore! There are more monkey species in Brazil than anywhere else in the world. The Christ the Redeemer Statue in Rio de Janeiro is one of the world's great symbols of Christianity. It has the most famous carnival festival in the world. What's not to like?

On the other hand, the Canon del Agua Ranch has harsh winters. Howling winds. Almost no other human beings besides herself and Pete. No beaches, no rain forests, no carnivals, nothing resembling a world symbol or icon.

So, what did my mother do?

She took the bull by the horns, of course. She submitted my father's resume and a letter of application to the Swift Meat Packing Company, which had placed the ad.

She sent it in without my dad's knowledge.

Imagine my father's surprise when a letter came from Swift, asking him to come up to Chicago to interview for some ranch managing job in . . . Brazil, of all places.

I can imagine the conversation going something like this:

"Um . . . Mary Lee?"

"Yes?"

"What's this letter from Swift saying I have a job interview with them?"

"Oh! Let me see that!" She would have likely ripped the letter from his hand and pored over every detail, a big grin on her face.

"Yes!"

"You mind explaining what this is about?"

"It's about *us,* Pete! Getting out of this hellhole. Living someplace *adventurous.* A place where things actually *happen* and we're not surrounded by a million acres of *nothing.*"

She'd explain how she came across the ad in the *Cattleman's Quarterly* and sent in his resume.

"Swift is a very reputable company. And besides, they're offering us a free visit to Chicago to do the interview! At the very least, we could take some time off from this place and go see a city we've never seen. It'll be our little adventure! You can always say no. But you might just like it."

My father would have shrugged and agreed with her. He was not one to rock the boat. But, secretly, I'm guessing he would not have been truly interested in going to work for Swift, no matter how reputable they were. He felt he had a great job already, and he was in position to take over for Buck when he retired. And the thought of having to tell Buck he was taking a new job and moving to Brazil was not an appealing one.

I think he looked at it this way: They would go to Chicago. He would see the Union Stock Yard, the operation that had made Chicago, in the poet Carl Sandburg's words, the "hog butcher for the world." Chicago was the center of the American meatpacking industry. Why not take a free trip up there, talk to the Swift executives, see the Stock Yard, take in the sights of the City of Big Shoulders, as Sandburg had called it?

And then, if Swift offered him a job, he could turn it down, and get on with his life as it was.

And so they left me with a ranch hand's family and went to Chicago, taking the train from Las Vegas across the Kansas plains, through the Missouri woodlands and prairies, and up through the heartland of Illinois, passing by its corn and bean fields, its hog and cattle farms, its prairies and towns, until they finally reached Chicago.

They went without telling John Tatton, the man who owned both the Salt Creek Ranch and the Canon del Agua Ranch, Buck on one ranch, my dad on the other. And they went without telling Buck Emmert, not wanting him to blow a gasket or cause any unnecessary anger or angst.

After all, this was just an exploratory trip, my dad told himself. Likely nothing would come of it.

My mom was in paradise. They were wined and dined in Chicago. They were put up in a good hotel, taken to fine restaurants, and even—to my mother's delight—got to ride in a taxi, which she had never done before.

Mom loved the whole experience, in part because she was deemed by Swift to be an integral part of the interview process. The executives explained at dinner that first night that it was just as important that the wife was on board with the move, particularly when it was an international one.

"If the wife doesn't like the situation, then what happens is things begin to fall apart, and even if the husband likes it over there, for the sake of the marriage, they end up moving back to the States," one executive said.

She convinced them that she was a hundred percent behind the move—that she, indeed, was the one who had initiated the correspondence with Swift.

The executive looked at my mom and dad, who merely raised his eyebrows as if to say, "Buddy, you don't know the half of it."

"So, you like the idea of moving to Brazil?" the Swift man asked her.

"I don't like it," she replied. "I *love* it!"

The two Swift men exchanged glances and grins.

"Okay, then," one said. "How's your steak?"

"Not quite as good as ours at home, but it'll do," my mom said, winking.

The job opening was not just with Swift. Swift had partnered with King Ranch, the largest ranch in Texas at 825,000 acres. King consisted of four large divisions: the Santa Gertrudis, the Laureles, the Encino, and the Norias. King Ranch was made a National Historic Landmark in 1961, just a few years after my parents' trip to Chicago.

The ranch, founded by Captain Richard King and Gideon K. Lewis in 1853, grazed cattle, horses, sheep, and goats. (Kingsville, by the way, was named after Richard King.) Eventually, Brahman bulls were crossed with Beef Shorthorns to produce Santa Gertrudis cattle, the first American breed of beef cattle. Not surprisingly, Richard King took his own bull by the horns; he was born in New York City, indentured at the age of nine to a jeweler in Manhattan, but the life of a city jeweler was no more for him than the life of a New Mexico ranch wife was for my mother. So, at age eleven, King stowed away on a ship bound for Mobile, Alabama. The crew liked his spunk, trained him as a navigator, and he became a steamboat pilot at the age of sixteen. He formed a steamboat company with a few other partners and was active in the Cotton Road trade during the Civil War, selling Confederate cotton through Mexico after the government blocked ports through which the cotton was normally sold. He holed up in Mexico in 1863 when his ranch was attacked by Union soldiers, and stayed there until he was given a letter of amnesty by President Lincoln nearly two years later; he then began acquiring the land that became King Ranch.

My father, of course, had high regard for the legendary King Ranch. When he learned of the partnership between Swift and King, it only piqued his interest.

During the dinner with the Swift executives, Pete was told that one thing Swift was interested in was seeing how well the Santa Gertrudis cattle could do in a tropical climate. They also wanted to introduce the quarter horse to Brazil. While the business relationship was indeed a partnership between Swift and King, Swift would be the company more directly involved in the ranch operations in Brazil, with King providing the expertise needed to run cow-calf operations and to improve the herds through stock breeding.

"We've been down in Brazil forty-some years," one Swift guy explained. "We've got the ranches and the slaughterhouse in São Paulo down there. We just need people with some ranching experience and savvy to run the ranches."

"Pete Emmert was born to be a cowboy," my mother said, earning a withering glance from her husband. "Did you know he rode a horse back and forth to school every day?"

The two company men smiled. "No, we did not," one said.

"Don't mind her," my dad said. "Tell me more about the operation down in Brazil."

The men continued the conversation. King Ranch wants to do a cow-calf operation, they said. That hasn't been our forte. We've just bought the steers cheap, fattened them, and shipped them off to the slaughterhouse. The pastures are over-grazed. They're in bad shape. We need someone who knows how to care for the pastures as well as the herds. Do you understand what we're getting at?

My dad did understand. He told them his knowledge and experience with keeping pastures lush and fertile, how to manage the land. What types of grasses would thrive best in a tropical climate. He had done his homework.

The Swift men nodded their heads. They were impressed.

A waiter brought coffee and dessert. The conversation continued, with each passing minute bringing more excitement to my mother. She knew they were on to something big, something life changing. She knew my dad was their man.

She just hoped they knew it, too.

While in Chicago, Swift took my dad out to the Union Stock Yard. The Yards opened in 1865, and from that point through the mid-1920s, processed more meat than anywhere else in the world. In its first thirty-five years of existence, about 400 million livestock were butchered within the Yards. By 1900, the Yards had about 25,000 employees, covered 475 acres, and produced about 82 percent of the nation's meat. By 1921, the Yards employed 40,000 people and was pumping half a million gallons of water from the Chicago River daily into the stockyards. The Yards was such a huge operation that the city had to permanently reverse the flow of the Chicago River in 1900 to keep the sewage from flowing into Lake Michigan and contaminating the city's drinking water.

To my dad, visiting the Yards was like stepping on hallowed ground.

He toured the Yards via the long, wooden walkways above the pens—two hundred acres of pens, each pen holding about one hundred head of cattle, which would be sent down the runways to the slaughterhouse when their time came. It was an amazing and immense operation, one that my dad put to use once he got to Brazil.

When the stockyard tour was finished, my parents went on a different sort of tour, one of the city. Because the stockyards were on the south side of Chicago, along the Chicago River, they started their tour on the South Side, notoriously poor and black. Mom had seen African Americans before, but not in the numbers she did in Chicago. They got to ride up Lake Shore Drive, see Navy Pier, Michigan Avenue with all its wonderful and glorious shopping on the Magnificent Mile, and other landmarks in the city. Funny that for my dad, heaven was the Stock Yards; for my mom, it was the Magnificent Mile.

Back home in New Mexico, they went about their business. Dad was intrigued by the possibility of working for the Swift-King operation, but did what his father had taught him to do since he was old enough to hold a hammer in his hand: get to work. Do the work that was in front of you, that needed to get done.

My mom, meanwhile, was growing more restless by the day.

"When do you think they'll let us know?" she pouted.

"When they're ready to let us know," my dad answered.

"What's taking them so long?"

"I don't know. You want to call them up and find out?"

My father no doubt felt a quick pang of regret at saying that; he likely feared Mom would take him up on his sarcastic challenge. She didn't.

Luckily for them both, they heard just a few days later, by certified mail. Swift hadn't let her down. They had tabbed my father as their man. Would he be so kind as to give a response?

Mom let out a yelp of joy and exultation. It might have been loud enough for the Swift executives to hear in Chicago, but just in case, Mom and Dad responded by mail: yes, they would be delighted to take over Laranja Doce (Sweet Orange) Ranch.

By this time, Dad had warmed up to the possibility, though he would have been fine had he not been offered the job. But the idea of moving to a new country, of working for the famous King Ranch corporation and facing new challenges, had begun to grow on him.

Of course, a more immediate challenge facing him was telling Buck that he was leaving. Not just New Mexico, but the country. He had to tell ranch owner John Tatton, too, but that would be far easier.

He chose to tell Tatton first, because Tatton was his boss and deserved to know before anyone else. And, yes, because Tatton was less likely to explode.

Dad hated to use the phone—he had a phobia about it, in fact, and used it as little as possible—but he had to call Tatton, who lived in Texas.

He called Tatton and told him he'd been to Chicago recently. That he'd interviewed for a job with Swift-King. Tatton was surprised.

"You've hardly been in New Mexico," he said.

"That's true. But Mary Lee, well, she's not exactly thrilled with the winters up here in the mountains . . ."

"So where's the job?"

"Brazil."

A moment of shocked silence. Then: "*Brazil*?"

Dad told Tatton about the opportunity as it was presented to him in Chicago.

"Well, Pete, that's a pretty big move, isn't it?"

"It is, Mr. Tatton. And I'm pretty excited about it, though I've enjoyed working for you. And I know my dad has, too."

Tatton asked if he had signed a contract yet, and for how long. Pete replied he had signed a two-year contract.

"Well, we were hoping you'd take over for your father once he retires," Tatton said. "And that still could happen. You could go down there for your two years and come back."

Tatton talked about the timing of the move and some ranch particulars. Then he paused a moment and chuckled.

"It just struck me you'll be raising your little one in Brazil, at least for a few years. What's her name again?"

"Elizabeth."

"Well, it should be a grand adventure for her. It's probably good she's going down there before she's learned English yet."

"Yeah, I guess so. Hey, Mr. Tatton, can I ask you one favor? Could you not tell Buck anything? I, uh, haven't told him yet."

"I'm sure it will come as a shock to him," Tatton said. He wished my dad well, told him he'd be a success at whatever he did and wherever he did it, and hung up.

That was the easy conversation.

Then came Buck.

My father's hands were sweaty when he finally conjured up the nerve, a few days later, to call his dad. He'd had a drink, or two, to calm his nerves. Not that it helped any.

"Buck?"

"Yes." Buck always had slightly irritated tone in his voice when talking on the phone. Especially when answering such an obvious question.

"I, uh, wanted to tell you something."

"Okay." Neither was Buck very chatty on the phone. My dad came by his aversion to the phone honestly.

Dad cleared his throat. "We're leaving New Mexico."

A slight pause. Then: "What are you talking about?"

The cat was not only out of the bag; it was running amok. No capturing it and stuffing it back into the bag.

Dad took a deep breath and plunged in. "We're moving to Brazil. To take over a ranch down there. It's a joint venture between Swift Meat Packing and King Ranch." Dad hoped the mention of the two venerable companies—especially King Ranch—would somewhat ameliorate Buck's rancor.

John Tatton had called it right: Buck was dumfounded. But not for long.

He pulled from his son the basic details of the move, asked him why on earth he would consider such a thing anyway, and lambasted him for moving so far away. Dad wisely didn't mention that Mom had set things in motion by applying for the position without his knowledge. Not that it would have surprised Buck, or made him think less of his daughter-in-law.

Buck told my dad all the reasons it was a dumb move and asked him if he could undo it.

Dad countered by saying it was a very good two-year contract, it included furnished housing and food, he would be paid in US dollars and have great medical insurance, and he would even be given a car and a driver.

"I thought you knew how to drive," Buck said drolly.

"It's a done deal. We're going," Dad replied.

"When?"

"Three weeks."

He could hear Buck fuming. "Don't expect us to be coming down there to visit you," Buck said. Then he hung up.

Dad sighed. At least that part was over. The rest of the complicated and long move—with an infant in tow—seemed like a piece of cake to him.

In the world according to Mary Lee Emmert, life *is* like bull wrangling. And she had just wrangled her bull all the way from New Mexico to Brazil.

CHAPTER 3

GOODBYE AMERICA, HELLO BRAZIL

IT'S AMAZING HOW SIMPLE A MAJOR MOVE can be once the decision is made and any major hurdles—such as telling someone like Buck Emmert—have been leapt over.

I was only nine months old when we boarded a ship in November 1958 in the Port of Houston and made the two-week-long journey to the Port of Santos, which was 6,740 nautical miles away. At the Port of Santos, we were met by Swift employees who drove us to São Paulo, about a two-hour drive from the port. São Paulo at the time was home to 3.5 million people, which was four times the population of all of

Pete, Mary Lee, Betinha, Del Sul, 1958. Author collection.

Mary Lee Emmert (mother) and Betinha on Delta Steamship Lines, Del Sul 1958. Author collection.

New Mexico when we left what my mother would call "that godforsaken state."

In São Paulo my parents met with company executives, who welcomed them to Brazil, asked about their trip, and tried to help them get a bit of a start on acclimating to a foreign country—one whose primary language was Portuguese and whose culture was significantly different from anything either of my parents had experienced. Brazil has a wide cultural mix, being heavily influenced by its colonization by the Portuguese empire and by the African and Indigenous American traditions, as we would come to learn. The food, religion, music, and dance were all greatly impacted by the Africans and the Indigenous tribes who populated the land, particularly the areas by the coast and rivers.

The Swift-King ranches that my dad would come to manage—most of which were relatively close together—were a good 350 miles from São Paulo. That journey would have been either a long and bumpy ride, much of it on gravel or dirt roads, whose conditions would depend on recent rainfalls and mudslides, or it would have been a fourteen-hour

Mary Lee, Betinha, Mr. Folly, Rio de Janeiro, 1958. Mr. Folly was an employee of Swift and greeted the Emmert family in Brazil. Author collection.

train ride. Thankfully, Swift put us on one of their company planes and flew us to Bartira Ranch. We learned later that this was quite the privilege, as typically those planes were reserved for the general manager of the ranches and used primarily for emergencies. (There were five Swift-King ranches, all near Presidente Prudente, a thriving city in the state of São Paulo. Each ranch had a manager, and a general manager oversaw all five ranches. My dad was hired originally to manage Laranja Doce Ranch.)

Bartira Ranch was the headquarters ranch where the general manager lived. Upon arriving at Bartira, we were brought to the general manager's house. He was as ancient as I was young, a no-nonsense widower whose presence was softened by his daughter, who lived with him on the ranch and managed the household.

Because Brazil is in the southern hemisphere, it was summertime; the daughter offered my parents ice tea and cooed a bit over me. I was not yet walking, but was close; my mother set me on the floor and I crawled around as the general manager, Monte Irwin, talked to my dad (he saw no need to address my mother) about the ranch operations in general, and in particular about Laranja Doce. He grilled my dad on his experience, but he was not unkind. He was simply gruff and blunt. As had been explained to my dad in Chicago, Irwin reiterated the company's desire to develop the Santa Gertrudis cattle—the cattle that had been bred on King Ranch in Texas specifically in hopes of finding a breed that could flourish in tropical climates, such as Brazil's. That was the big project on all the Swift-King ranches; it bonded all the ranches' managers and employees as they worked on this potential game-changer in the beef industry. That was my father's explicit mission; that's why he signed his original two-year contract with Swift.

When he was a teenager, Monte Irwin moved to Argentina from the United States to work in the Anglo-Argentine cattle industry, which was one of the largest in the world. He started at the bottom, became a cattle buyer, and continued to work his way up with Swift, which was very big in Argentina. Swift eventually transferred Monte to Brazil to run their ranches in the western portion of the State of São Paulo. Swift would buy cattle not only in São Paulo, but in Mato Grosso as well; the latter state was, back in the '60s, Brazil's version of the wild Wild West.

Monte would load up the ranches with these cattle until they were ready to be shipped to the packing plant near the city of São Paulo. He often overgrazed the pastures, and consequently the ranches were not in very good shape when Dad got down there. Pretty quickly, Dad became concerned with the quality of the grass on the ranches, and he would come to greatly improve the pastures.

Of greater interest to me, though, were Monte's two daughters, Marilyn and Jean. Monte was widowed, and Marilyn had just the right polish, charm, and sophistication to act as hostess for the many business and social events that Monte, as general manager, needed to hold. I absolutely adored Marilyn, who learned her charm while in Argentina, which was under British influence at the time. She brought the consummate lady's touch to the ranches, as she influenced the décor, the making of beds, and the proper serving of dinners.

After the meeting at Bartira, my parents and I were driven to Laranja Doce, which was about fifteen miles from Bartira. Brasilandia Ranch was larger than Laranja and adjacent to both Laranja Doce and Bartira. Formosa and Mosquito were the other two ranches owned by the Swift-King partnership.

Laranja Doce—as with all the ranches—had a *sede,* or main house, for the manager and his family. The division of duty was stereotypical: the husband ran the ranch, the wife ran the household and oversaw the garden and the domestic help. Upon arriving at the ranch—which, again, like all the others, was fully furnished—my mother found herself in charge of a gardener and three young Brazilian maids who cooked

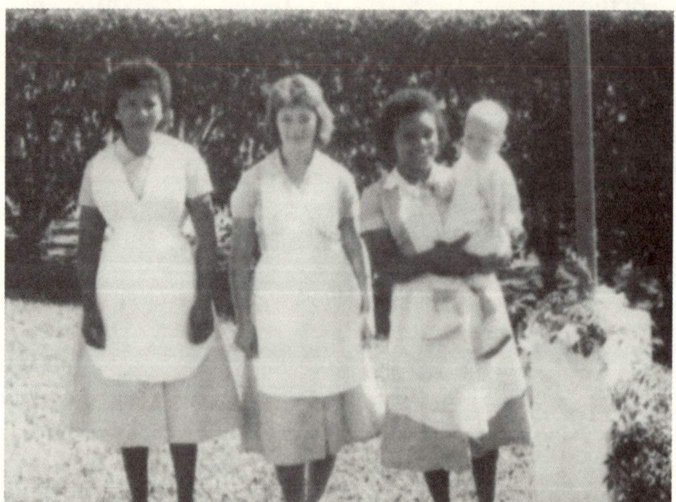

Astrogilda, Angelina, Maria, and Elizabeth (Betinha) 1959, Laranje Doce. Author collection.

and cleaned (and who only spoke Portuguese, which proved to be a bit of a challenge for Mom).

Believe me, my mother loved having others cook and clean for her! And in later years, as I grew older and my brothers and sister came along, my mother acquired nannies and tutors as well. She was in her element as a general, barking out orders, telling her domestic help to do this, do that. She was a queen bee, thriving in her hive.

But what drained a bit of enjoyment from that queen bee status was the ever-present language barrier. She had trouble understanding the help, and the help had trouble understanding her. My dad knew Spanish reasonably well, and there are similarities between Spanish and Portuguese, so he fared better. My mother, on the other hand, didn't know a lick of Spanish, Portuguese, or anything else other than English, though she picked up a few cuss words in Portuguese and put them to good use. (To her credit, she tried: she carried an English-to-Portuguese dictionary with her wherever she went. It was a well-thumbed book. Too bad Google and smartphones didn't exist back then!)

Luckily for her, as we kids grew up, we were bilingual, so we helped with the translation—and she did pick up the language, certainly, as the years rolled on.

I do recall, however, many occasions when she would end up throwing a fit because she felt she was speaking perfectly understandable Portuguese, but the help or shop owners or whomever she was addressing would frown and hold their hands out in front of them, palms upward, and say "Eu não entendo" (*I don't understand*). Which would drive my mother crazy. She didn't realize she spoke with a horribly stilted accent that undoubtedly was comically funny to those on the receiving end, though they wouldn't dare let on in front of my mother for fear of being challenged to a duel. The Queen Bee was nothing if not feisty and cantankerous.

"What's *wrong* with these people?" she would fume. "Can't they understand their own *language*?"

Of course, it would never dawn on her that she was the source of the misunderstanding.

One time, when I was a teenager, I remember being with her in Presidente Prudente at a café, where she was ordering a sandwich. The waiter asked her if she would like it *quente* (hot) or *frio* (cold).

A bit frustrated, she repeated her order.

He politely repeated his question about how she wanted it.

In growing exasperation, she repeated her order again, this time talking louder and enunciating to perfection (in her mind).

The waiter cleared his throat, became slightly uneasy, and asked once more if she would like her order *quente* or *frio.*

She clenched her hands. Her eyes bulged nearly out of their sockets. Through gritted teeth she repeated her order once more, looking at the poor man as if she were daring him to do anything other than turn around, put the damn order in, and bring her the damn sandwich.

The waiter, still trying to maintain his professional dignity, looked pleadingly at me.

I, of course, could have stepped in long before this, but I was enjoying seeing my mother lose it yet again.

I nodded to the waiter—*I have this*—and turned to my mother. "Mom, he's just asking you if you want your sandwich hot or cold." I concentrated hard on not laughing, though I couldn't wait to get back home to tell my siblings about her latest travails with the Portuguese language.

"Shut up!" she said, red-faced—probably partly from anger and partly from embarrassment. "I know that! Just tell him I want it hot. *Hot.*" She turned to the beleaguered waiter and shouted, "Cinquenta!"

I bust a gut laughing. The poor man turned to me again, confused.

"*Quente,*" I said. "She means *quente.*" (Meaning, *hot.*)

In her exasperation, she had yelled "*Fifty*!" at him.

If ever a group of people stuck out like sore thumbs in a foreign land, it was us. But we weren't alone. On four of the five ranches, the managers were not native Brazilians, and that, plus the common goal of developing the Santa Gertudis breed in Brazil, bound us ranch families tightly together. We ended up good friends with many of the other managers' families. When we'd venture into Presidente Prudente for shopping, entertainment, or, later, my piano lessons, we received lots of stares from the citizens, who weren't used to seeing many pasty-faced white folk from up north.

But kids in particular have an ability to break through cultural and other barriers, and it helped immensely that we learned Portuguese as our first language. I had none of the language barriers my mother faced. I made friends and had wonderful experiences growing up in Brazil. Those experiences shaped who I am today, and I wouldn't trade them for anything.

Swift had owned Laranja Doce for many years, so the land was largely cleared of trees. The land was fertile, requiring no fertilizer to establish pastures, but the pastures had been overgrazed, and one of Dad's first challenges was to reform the pastures. Part of that challenge was dealing with the earth termites and saúva ants that had claimed the land as theirs, creating extensive networks of underground labyrinths that would have to be tilled and chewed up before the pastures could be replanted with healthy grasses.

The termites built structures that looked like stalagmites—long, tapering columns about four to six feet tall and about a foot in diameter at the base. When these columns were knocked down and the ground was tilled, the termites were taken care of. The saúva ants, on the other hand, would tunnel underground and create huge, dug-out areas. If a tractor ran over one of these areas just right (well, just *wrong*), it would sink into the earth and have to be pulled out.

To kill off these ants, people with bags or buckets of granular insecticide would be sent out into the pastures to drop the sugar-coated granules in the paths of the ants. (The ants' working paths could stretch out for hundreds of feet.) The ants would carry the sweet poison back

Pete Emmert, Betinha, Fazenda Laranja Doce, 1959. Author collection.

to the hive, share the yummy stuff with their pals, and they would be taken care of for that year. But this was a battle that had to be fought annually.

You have to hand it to him: my dad had guts. He primarily went to Brazil to please my mom; he never would have gone on his own. To pick up and move about seven thousand miles away, with a young wife and an infant daughter, to a country where he didn't know the language, took courage. Add to that the immense challenges of clearing the pastures and planting grass and learning on the fly how to raise Santa Gertrudis under tropical conditions—all the while trying to learn a new language within a new culture and adjust to a very different way of life—was a lot to bite off for a young man only recently out of college.

But my dad was never one to shy away from a challenge. He learned that from the master, Buck Emmert. Buck had taught him two things: Always be working. And do the work that's in front of you.

The work that was in front of my father was getting the land in shape to support the Santa Gertrudis that would be bred on the ranch. So, he and his twenty or so ranch hands set about clearing the land of the scrub and thickets and weeds. They cleared the land with two Caterpillar D8s—large, track-type tractors that dragged "ripper" chains behind them. These chains were about six inches in diameter and two hundred to three hundred feet long, and they churned up the soil and destroyed the underground labyrinths of the termites. Unlike in the US, there was no respite from the insects; the winters in Brazil weren't harsh enough to kill them off. Yes, he had grown up on a ranch. But ranches in Brazil, he quickly learned, were different from ranches in South Texas.

They would use the D8s to push the brush and thickets into big piles, which they would later burn. This work also scattered numerous snakes that were nesting in the brush. They also used Agent Orange, an herbicide known for its use during the Vietnam War, which not only damaged whatever land it was used on, but also was quite toxic to people who were exposed to the deadly chemical, which has been documented to cause leukemia, Hodgkin's lymphoma, and other kinds of cancer. I always wondered if my dad was affected by the use of the Agent Orange that was used to defoliate the trees they were clearing; he died of rectal cancer at the young age of fifty-eight. He was also a heavy cigarette smoker, which many people were at the time, and that didn't help his health any, either.

My dad grew up observing his dad work on the ranch, and as soon as he was big enough to hold a hammer, you can believe my dad was put to work. But he didn't learn how to just work *hard* from Buck; he learned how to work *smart.* My dad acquired keen observational and listening skills that served him well throughout his life, and that were critical to his success on the Swift-King ranches in Brazil, which he ended up managing for twenty-three years. As I mentioned, Brazil represented a whole new way of life for us, and that included ranching. If my father had been bullheaded about his way of ranching and tried to ranch as he had in Texas and New Mexico, he wouldn't have lasted long.

But he watched, asked questions, listened to answers, and learned. For example, one day he observed a horse with a bellyache being treated with a tea colloquially called *cura curso* (literally, "healing course"), and he saw that the tea, made from the bark of a tree, worked. So, instead of using a prescribed antitoxin, he learned about the tea, he asked to see the tree the bark came from, and he used that treatment in similar future instances.

When he witnessed kerosene being added to the salt trough to treat foot-and-mouth disease—a highly contagious viral disease that can be devastating to livestock, and which is pretty much nonexistent in the US but prevalent in South America—he explored why kerosene was used, how effective and safe it was, and precisely how much was added to the troughs. He talked to other ranchers who had used this peculiar treatment and when he was sure it was safe and effective, he stored that away in his mind for future use, if necessary.

Here was this *Americano* with a college degree who would essentially sit at the feet of these ranch hands—*campieros*—and learn from them. He respected them, their knowledge, and their traditions. He never presented himself as superior to them, though it was clear to all involved that he was their boss. He knew that their years of experience on Brazilian ranches was an invaluable source of wisdom for him to tap into.

And that tapping went deep, in part because my dad was so even-tempered, respectful of others' abilities and knowledge, and able to galvanize a team of illiterate but highly intelligent *campieros.* When my mother flew off the handle, we all knew it was second nature for her; if my father ever lost his temper, there was a good reason for it, and that reason was a long time in the making, because he had a very long fuse.

Would he ever get mad at one of his ranch hands? Of course. What workplace doesn't have disagreements or arguments? But he would always ask for an explanation first—for example, why a person didn't carry out a task as directed. If, after the explanation, he believed someone's action, or inaction, deserved a dressing down, then he delivered that dressing down, but always with a controlled voice. He could speak sternly and yet evenly; he never yelled or raged at anyone. Thus, the *campieros* greatly respected my father, and were willing to work hard for him. (Perhaps this is why my dad's nickname among the *campieros* was *Pé de Anjo,* which means "Foot of an Angel." My mom did not fare as well with the moniker given her: *Jararaca,* which means "Pit Viper Snake.")

The *campieros* were generally a rough-hewn breed. Many of them were migrant workers who came from Brazil's drought-stricken northeast, moving to wherever they could find work. Their way of settling disputes among themselves was often through physical means—fistfights or occasionally through knives. The world they grew up in was one of poverty, constant lack of resources, and violence. It was all they knew. It takes a long time for a man in these circumstances to trust another man, and it takes just a moment to break that trust.

For my father to develop the trust and the relationships that he had with these men is nothing short of remarkable. For him to build a team of *campieros* that worked cohesively and trusted each other is even more extraordinary.

There was a rhythmic flow to these *campieros*; some would drift away and others would drift in. From everything I've heard from our neighbors on the other Swift-King ranches, those ranch hands left better off than they had come, and they left with respect and admiration for their *patrão Americano*—their American boss—Pete Emmert.

You will recall that my mother was quite the socialite. She wanted people around her to socialize and party with as often as possible. That was one of the many reasons she hated the ranch in New Mexico: it was barren not just in terms of land, but of people.

Pete, Betinha, Mary Lee, 1960. Author collection.

Not so in Brazil. Four of the five Swift-King ranches—Laranja Doce, Bartira, Formosa, and Brasilandia—were close together. Mosquito, the fifth ranch, was a bit farther away. But the men who managed these ranches were in constant communication with each other, because they were all on the same Swift-King team, all working toward the same end. That said, there was some underlying tension among the managers, because anyone hired in the US—such as my father was—received two significant perks that managers hired in Brazil, whether they were American or not, did not receive. Those hired in the US were paid part of their salary in US dollars and got paid home leave every year for a month (this was later reduced to every other year); those hired in Brazil were paid in cruzeiros, a currency that was constantly devaluating, and received normal vacation, but no home leave.

Still, the managers' families bonded well, and spent most weekends together at informal get-togethers or planned parties. The couples would get together on one ranch or the other, eat, drink, share stories about what was happening on their ranch, joke, listen to music, and generally have a good time.

This, of course, delighted my mother, who found herself in her element at these gatherings. She lived for these respites on the weekends—a time when she could fling her English-to Portuguese dictionary in a corner and go out and talk with people whose first language was *English*. She made some lifelong friends among the men and women at the other ranches. And it was great for us kids, too, as we had friends to play with, though we also made friends with the kids who lived with their parents in the colonies on the ranches that housed the ranch *empregados* (employees).

Duncan Renwick was just an eighteen-year-old kid from England when he was hired on to work as an apprentice at Mosquito. You can imagine an eighteen-year-old coming halfway across the world to work on a Brazilian ranch had a bit of devil-may-care in him, and Duncan certainly had a zest for living life to its fullest (and, at times, zaniest). I recall one of our weekend parties was a costume affair, and Duncan arrived wrapped in a cowhide and bellowing like a cow in heat. Other males were dressed in maids' uniforms. I looked forward to these parties as much as my mother did; there was always excitement in the air as Friday arrived and the weekend plans came into full swing.

After a year at Laranja Doce, my father was transferred to Bartira to manage that ranch, taking over for one who would become a good family friend, Ed Lasater, another fellow Texan who came from a prominent ranching family. (Ed was returning to Texas but would come back to Brazil to take over one of the ranches again.) The Swift-King operation was testing my dad, I think, to see what his capacity was for managing, knowing his experience in Texas and seeing how that would translate

Pete Emmert (father), Elizabeth (Betinha), Jimmy Emmert (Betinha's brother), Mary Lee Green Emmert (mother), Bartira manager house. 1960. Author collection.

down in Brazil. Also, the general manager for all five ranches lived at Bartira, and his ranching background was not as strong as my dad's. So my dad was shifted to Bartira the first time that Ed Lasater left for Texas.

I was not quite two yet when we moved to Bartira, so obviously I don't remember that time—but we also spent time there when I was a teenager, and from those days I remember the ranch well.

We spent the next two years at Bartira, which was fifteen miles northeast of the town of Rancharia. Each ranch was near a little town, but the main city was Presidente Prudente, which was a good forty miles away from Bartira. The last time I was in Rancharia, a handful of years ago, it had retained its quaintness: one movie theater, an ice cream parlor, a library, and a whorehouse. I guess you could say it offered education and entertainment of various sorts, all wrapped into one tiny township.

Speaking of the library, my mother was a driving force behind its creation. She believed a library would be a great asset for the community, and had to push hard for it, because township funds were never too abundant. Once the library was finally built, the town had no money for books, so it housed tables, chairs, and newspapers. However, it was the tallest building in the town and a source of pride for its citizens. Leave it to my mother, the English teacher, to champion literacy in Rancharia.

I wish she would have championed healthcare instead. The town's citizens referred to the tiny hospital as the butcher shop, and my sister Theresa experienced firsthand what they were talking about. She broke her arm when she was twelve years old and the doctor set it incorrectly. (Thankfully, she went back and got it reset by a capable doctor.) Arms must have been a mystery to the doctors there; our gardener's son broke his arm, but when he came home from the hospital, he was still crying in pain, and his parents realized the doctor had put the cast on the wrong arm. It apparently didn't take a lot of training or education to become a nurse there; you just showed up, did bedpan duty for a while, and when the need arose—which it always would, because the hospital was short-staffed—you were promoted to nurse. One of our maids became a nurse that way.

My mother, I will say, was unfairly named Pit Viper. In addition to being instrumental in bringing a library to Rancharia, she also went to extremes to help an orphanage in town. She arranged for Swift-King to deliver leftover carcasses from the weekly slaughters; the nuns received the free meat with tears in their eyes. Mom also had a yearly Christmas party at our house for the twenty to thirty orphans, who would spend most of the day eating, playing games, and swimming, with some of the older kids riding a few of our tamer horses. We would do a *churrasco* (barbecue) for lunch, and Mom made sure to pack in plenty of ice cream and soda before the kids arrived. Sometimes we'd have *queijo prato* (literally, "plate-shaped cheese"), a soft Brazilian cheese that was originally made by Danish immigrants in the 1920s. The orphans were most excited about the food—it was a feast for them, one that many of the older ones anticipated for many weeks before the big day finally arrived. Mom would also buy shoes and clothes for the kids, and she made sure that every child went home with some sort of prize from the game playing.

It took about thirty minutes of dirt-road driving from Rancharia to Bartira. The drive was scenic; we passed through other ranches and by a small dam and then past a three hundred-meter line of *Cieba pentrada* (kapok) trees, large majestic flowering trees that are native to Central and South America. When the trees were in bloom, their pink petals covered the road. I noticed on a recent visit back to Bartira, the town had cut down the trees to widen the road. Another reminder that everything changes.

When I was a girl, however, we would reach Bartira after driving down this petal-strewn road, passing a stream, and curving around a hill. Several steps led up to the open front porch of the *sede,* a long and spacious four-bedroom ranch house; inside, wooden floors ran the length of the house, which was furnished in good taste. The *sede* was separated from the bookkeeper's house by a eucalyptus grove, and had huge pine trees in the front yard. As with all the other ranches, it also

Mary Lee Emmert (mother), 1961. Author collection.

had maid quarters and a *churrasco* pit where we could barbecue some delicious beef, courtesy of the ranch's crossbreds (we would never, of course, consume the purebred Santa Gertrudis; they were only for breeding).

Another tasty treat we had in Brazil was mangoes. They were plentiful down there. I remember one time, Jimmy and Theresa and I rode our horses to the orchard in one of the ranch's colonies so we could steal some mangoes. The thrill of that sweet juice dribbling down our chins from the stolen fruit was incredible. We thought the colony's mangoes were far tastier than the ones in our own orchard.

Mom planted flowering trees along the side of the lane leading to our house; the shade from the trees would help the cattle cool down in the hot summer months. The ranch had an outdoor dining area, an airplane hangar and strip, three colonies of houses, a machine shop, and a big wooden house with vines taking it over; this was where the single men and any workers from other ranches would eat their meals of meat, rice, and beans.

The colonies' houses were separated by rank: The upper colony was occupied by those with the top jobs, such as the managers and foremen (*capatazes*); the lower two colonies would house the laborers and cowboys. Many of the colony houses had a pig in a fenced-in area; this pig would feast on all the kitchen leftovers. Chickens roamed free around the yards until they became that night's dinner.

During these early years in Brazil—in fact, pretty much for the duration—communication between my dad and Buck was through letter; Buck took care of Dad's bank accounts and investments in the US. Neither liked to talk on the phone, and neither would have wanted to spend what would have been an exorbitant amount of money back then to place a long-distance call, anyway. Letter was not only their preferred method for communicating; it was the norm back in those days. The art of letter writing has been totally submerged in this age of technology, where emails, texts, and social media have taken over. Pretty soon, parents are going to have to explain to their kids what "writing a letter" means, causing the kids to no doubt look horrified.

The art of penmanship is also largely lost, because people simply don't write enough to master it (or to care), but back then, my dad had amazing handwriting. He would write on super-thin airmail paper, keeping his correspondence businesslike, talking about the ranch, insurance, and finances.

My dad was paid about half in US dollars and half in Brazilian cruzeiros. He would have just put his American dollars in CDs or something pretty safe; he tended to be a worrier about money. My mom was more the risk-taker; she invested some of the money in stocks, and they did quite well with their investments.

My father was a meticulous record-keeper, which came in handy not only for insurance and tax purposes, but for the breeding of his Santa Gertrudis cattle. Such skills and attention to detail meant everything for the successful breeding and sales of Swift-King's prized cattle in Brazil.

The Swift executives apparently liked what they saw in my father. That's not only why they transferred him to Bartira; that's why they were only too happy to sign him to another two-year contract. Those two-year contracts kept rolling in over the years, and this Americano from Texas began to make a name for himself in the ranching industry in southeastern Brazil.

CHAPTER 4

NEXT STOP, MOSQUITO RANCH

IN 1961 DUNCAN RENWICK, who had been managing Mosquito Ranch, moved to Paraguay to run a ranch for an English outfitter. That left an opening at Mosquito Ranch, and Swift executives asked my father to fill it.

Mosquito was the largest of the five ranches, with more than thirty-four thousand acres, thirty thousand of which were pasture. The rest were in the jungle by the Paranapanema River. The ranch was the farthest removed from the other Swift-King ranches, at least a two-hour drive south of Bartira, near the town of Narandiba, São Paulo. For these reasons it required a responsible and savvy rancher who could autonomously run the ranch. Swift had groomed my dad for that position.

So, we—now a family of four, as my brother Jimmy had been born the previous year—moved to Mosquito, where we would live for the next nine years (I was two years old when we moved to Mosquito and eleven when we left it). This ranch—named not for the pesky insect, but for a river of Minas Gerais state in southeastern Brazil—was owned by King Ranch and was its premier "show ranch."

Mosquito was not only the largest ranch; it was the most unsettled. A Hatfield-McCoy type of boundary feud was ongoing between the ranchers and the squatters, who consisted of former slaves, Africans, and *caipiras* (country hicks, who had their own dialect and brand of music)

Elizabeth (Betinha), 1965. Author collection.

who were living in the swamp area and jungle near the river. (The Brazilian government mandated that a certain percent of the land—about 5 percent, in the State of São Paulo's case—remain native jungle.) When Swift-King bought the land for the ranch, ranch employees worked to clear the land on the edges of the jungle. The Brazilian government wanted to protect some of the virgin jungle around Mosquito, but the exact border was in dispute. I learned later that ranch hands before our time there took to shooting rifles in the air in an attempt to scare off the squatters.

The main house on Mosquito was the newest of the houses we lived in on any of the ranches. It was a beautiful home with large windows in the living room looking out on the pastures. The living room and dining room were separated by a double-sided fireplace, our only source of warmth during the winter, as there was no central heating.

A screened-in porch spanned the dining and living rooms, and six bedrooms flanked either side of a long hall. Each bedroom had two doors: a glass door with venetian blinds and a wooden door. The hall was actually split in two by a glass door halfway down; the first half was for guests, the second half was for family.

As with the other ranch houses, this one was furnished. In fact, this was the best furnished of all. We had leather chairs and a pigskin couch in the living room and a sturdy oak dining room table and wooden dining chairs with cushioned leather seats.

At Mosquito we had a houseboy, Aniba, and five maids, including Judite, our cook, and Margarida, our nursemaid. Margarida's aunt, Conceicão, supervised the maids and was in charge of us kids when my parents traveled. A widow, she stayed with the family for twenty years.

The house sat high atop a hill, so we could see for miles around. The only access to it was a long dirt road that led to the state of Paraná, which was on the south side of the Paranapanema River. The river, one of the most important in the state of São Paulo, separates the states of Paraná and São Paulo. It was along this river that the squatters lived.

Buses would travel along this dirt road, and occasionally hoboes would wander up this road and ask us for food. The maid quarters were close to the road, which was lined with coffee bushes on one side and had a mango and jackfruit orchard on the other side. We also had banana plants and a large vegetable garden not far from this road. Further down the road was the horse pen and the tack room in which my dad made saddles. (This room had to be kept orderly, with bridles hung in the proper manner and place; sometimes, when we kids had finished riding, we were too tired or lazy to hang the bridles back up. Such mutinous behavior would incur the wrath of my father.)

Next to the maid quarters was a shed that housed the generator. Every night at ten o'clock, my dad would "pull the plug" on the main house's electricity to save fuel (the refrigerators and freezers were run on kerosene), and we were left with no electricity until the next morning.

Sometimes Dad would let us kids accompany him to turn off the generator. It was a relatively long walk, and we were always excited to go with him on these occasions. He'd have a huge flashlight in his hand to light our path, and we'd hear and see plenty of nocturnal animals on our way to the shed. Once Dad would shut the generator down, we were treated to a spectacular view of the sky, because the nearest manmade lights were about ten miles away. On our way back, we would often see giant cane toads. These are the world's largest toads, with adults averaging about four to six inches in length. Sometimes, to fend off predators (and bipeds returning to their house after shutting off the generator), these toads would puff up their lungs and lift their bodies off the ground to appear even larger than they were.

As we'd spot these toads or see the glowing eyes of other nocturnal animals, my brother Jimmy would sometimes sneak up behind me and scream "Ahh!" to scare me. Which it would, though I'd do my best to let on that I wasn't scared in the least.

Twice a year, my dad would drive the dirt road along the Paranapanema River through the *mato* (jungle) to see if any squatters were encroaching on the ranch property. The river was about twelve miles from the ranch. As I grew older, I would go along with him, but the river's current was swift and dangerous, pulling tree trunks into it as it flowed along. We saw sloths, river otter, parrots, and flightless rheas (related to ostriches) on our journeys along the river, and we were always on the lookout for the elusive *onca* (jaguar). We also came across spider monkeys and howler monkeys, the latter of which are aptly named; they sound almost spooky in their guttural howls, and would sound particularly creepy at night. I loved going along with my dad to see all the wildlife along the river and in the jungle.

My mother, naturally, was intrigued by the monkeys, and had the gardener plant some corn along the edge of the jungle so she could see them at night when we were down that way. We'd just turn on our headlights to watch them and listen to their strange howls. They are awake about nine hours a day, and the males spend essentially all of their waking hours howling.

If my dad saw evidence of a potential squatter trail, he would stop his jeep, get out his pistol, and investigate. One day he found a man living among the trees; the man had fashioned a hut in the root system of a large *figeira* (fig) tree; these trees are monstrously thick and large, and are native to Brazil. Dad had a sad but resolute look on his face as he evicted the man from the ranch territory.

My dad brought about many significant changes in ranch operations on not only Mosquito Ranch, but the other four ranches as well. One of those changes—and one that was not easy to convince the native Brazilian ranch hands to adopt—was the use of western saddles.

There was a big difference between the Brazilian and the western saddle.

The Brazilian saddle, back in the 1960s, did not have a horn (the part that is at the top of the pommel, in the front of the saddle; it provides support for the rider and a place for lassos and other equipment). The Brazilian saddle was light and comfortable, made of sheepskins sewn together. The rope the *campieros* (cowboys) used was attached to the horse's girth, allowing the horse to hold the steer. But Brazilian horses were smaller than western horses, and it was difficult for an eight-hundred-pound horse to hold a fifteen-hundred-pound steer. To compensate for this weight difference, Brazilian *campieros* would rope a steer and then run with the horse until the steer turned and slowed the horse, which would be straining and working hard against the steer's much heavier weight and strength. The *campieros* used a longer rope than is used with a western saddle, and they would also use a large post in the middle of the corral in helping to overcome the steer's strength advantage. By positioning themselves just right, the *campieros* could use both the post and the horse to try to wear down the steer. But it was a long process.

The western technique, on the other hand, focused on stopping the steer as quickly as possible—but to do so, you needed a stronger horse. And with a stronger—that is, larger—horse, you also were better off with a western saddle and shorter rope. The Brazilians were used to having the steer to their left or right, because if the steer was in front of them or behind them, the Brazilian saddle could easily be pulled off the horse. The western saddle was cinched under the front legs of the horse, though, and was much more secure than the Brazilian saddle.

A key point for my father in comparing the two saddles was this: the traditional Brazilian saddle rubbed on the horse's back, and the friction caused sores to form on the back. Dad hated this, and would chew the *campieros* out if he ever saw their horses with sores.

To combat this issue, my dad started a saddle shop on the ranch, training a *campiero* how to make western saddles, to be used with both the Brazilian horses and with the quarter horses that would be introduced to Swift-King ranches in the late '60s. Dad had gained some knowledge of how to fix saddles by watching Buck refurbish them over the years, and when we were back in Texas on leave, he would always visit the saddle shop on King Ranch, taking notes and pictures so he could teach the *campieros* how to make better saddles and other tack for the ranches in Brazil. (King Ranch also introduced saddle blankets to its Brazilian ranches, but these efforts were not as successful.)

The process of making a saddle was painstaking and slow. The saddle-maker would cut the hide for both sides of the saddle, making sure they were the same thickness. He would then get the cantle (the raised part at the back of the saddle) wet and wrap it in blankets to disperse the water evenly so he could later shape and tool it. He would form the ground seat, the swells, and the skirts, create the funnel-shaped horn, and wrap the stirrups. He patiently and skillfully went through numerous finely detailed steps before he ended up with a saddle that would help the rider be much more efficient in his roping and handling of steers.

That laborious process was followed by another not-so-easy chore: convincing the *campieros* that the western saddle was better for them. Some were reluctant to switch from their comfortable Brazilian saddles to this heavier and sturdier saddle. People get comfortable with how they've always done things, and don't readily embrace change. But the *campieros* had great respect for my father, and most adapted fairly quickly, being taught by my dad how to use the saddle horn and the shorter rope to rope steers. When those who were reluctant to do so saw how their fellow *campieros* were using the saddles to their advantage in handling the steers, they got on board with the new saddles.

In fact, over time, the use of the Brazilian saddle diminished and eventually was phased out, as King Ranch introduced the western saddle to the country. Today, Presidente Prudente is the capital of saddle-making in Brazil.

Dad also designed and built pens and dipping vats for the cattle to walk through to be treated for ticks and various diseases. The vats would be full of chemicals (and were later outlawed because of the chemicals used), and were narrow enough that the animals couldn't turn around; they were forced to walk through the water, which was nearly five feet deep and about fifty feet long. The bulls and larger cows would make quite a splash entering the vat, and the smell of manure mixed with the strong chemicals made for a pungent and unpleasant smell. Sometimes to get a cow through the chute and into the vat, you had to twist its tail from behind; that would get it moving forward. Several hundred head of cattle would go through the vat, one after the other, many bellowing their displeasure as they went.

When my brother Jimmy was six or seven years old, he slipped and fell into the plunge dip while watching the operation. He fell near the vat entrance, and dad pulled him out with a big hook, a *gancho*, which they used to poke the steers through the vat. Jimmy was soaked and upset, and they immediately stripped him down to his underwear and hosed him down with clean water. Dad then took him up to the house and told my mom what had happened. She, of course, was horrified.

"How much did he drink?" she shouted.

"I don't know. Did you drink any?" my dad asked Jimmy, who by this time was crying.

Jimmy shook his head, but that wasn't good enough for my mom.

"Make him throw up!" she demanded. "In case he drank any of it."

Based on how Jimmy entered the vat, my dad didn't think any went into Jimmy's mouth, but he also didn't think it was a bad idea to be on the safe side. So he induced vomiting by pressing down on Jimmy's tongue near his throat. Jimmy threw up and cried some more.

My dad then instituted the Jimmy Rule: when you were working the vat, you had to stay on the top platform, where you controlled the gates and had a railing to stand behind and hold onto.

My mother, by the way, loved working the gates. There were two gates, one to allow six cattle into the holding pen, the second to let them into the vat itself. It was a busy and active process, with lots of shouting—"Open number one!" "Close number one!" "Open number two!"—and my mom, I guess, liked the excitement of it all. But she wasn't strong enough to close a gate when a big steer pushed it open before she'd had time to close it. One time a steer pushed a gate open, allowing many more steers to crowd into the pen and angering my dad.

"Close the damn gate!" he yelled at her.

"I can't!" she shouted.

"Well then quit working the gate!"

This upset her enough that she started crying and stormed off, pouting. My dad later said he was sorry, and she grudgingly accepted his apology, but she never worked the gates again.

This was the only time I saw my parents argue in public.

The process I liked to watch more than the vat dipping was watching the steers being loaded onto the wooden rail cars in Narandiba, a tiny town about twenty miles from Mosquito Ranch, to go to the packing plant in São Paulo. The *campieros* would conduct a cattle drive to Narandiba, load the steers into pens next to the train station, and from there they would be loaded through chutes onto the train cars, starting from the last car, with the steers gradually herded toward the front cars, until the cars were filled. Heavy wooden boards bridged each car to the next, and the *campieros* would run along the tops of the open-roofed cars, herding the steers forward, and shouting to close the gate once a car was full. It was critical that they not let the steers turn around in the cars, or try to back out of the cars; that would result in a chaotic mess. The ranch had to hire additional workers from town to help with the task. I was allowed to watch from a safe distance, because the process could be dangerous; *campieros* lost fingers and suffered other injuries regularly when loading the steers. It was also a very long process; it took most of a day to load all the steers. Then the train would head to São Paulo at night, when it was cooler. I'm sure it was hot enough in those cars with all those steers stuck in there together.

But not every steer was herded onto a train bound for the slaughterhouse in São Paulo. Some "chosen few" were destined for our dining room table, and the tables of the ranch hands, those living in the ranch colonies.

We often had visitors stay with us—family friends, ranch officials, ranchers who were interested in this new breed of cattle that the Swift-King ranches were bringing in—and on Saturday mornings ("butcher day") I enjoyed watching the looks on their faces as we peered through the board slats of the slaughtering pen to witness the slaughtering of a steer.

My friends from the colony and I would make bets on which guest would be the most horrified by the event. Indeed, over the years, several of our guests fainted, or threw up, or cried out in disgust as the animal had its neck sliced to bleed out. The steer would then be hoisted on a pulley, and the butcher—a *campiero* during the week—would lance the heart, causing the blood to pump out and disappear down a large drain in the center of the floor. When the blood squirted out and pooled around the drain, this disgusted our guests even more.

The process is actually fascinating to watch—if you have the stomach for it. Once the steer has bled out, the butcher removes the hide and slices the carcass down the middle, removing the guts. The steer is washed out several times to keep the meat as clean as possible. The butcher would then cut each half of the steer into three pieces, because six pieces of a nine-hundred-pound animal is easier to handle than two halves. The pieces were then taken to the butcher shop, cut into smaller portions, and apportioned to the colony families, and the women from each family would take their meat home in large aluminum basins, *bacias,* often balancing the *bacias* on their heads.

Once the women got their meat home, they would cut it into thin strips, put them back in the *bacia,* and pour a liberal amount of coarse salt over them. They would then hang the strips from an outdoors clothesline made of barbed wire (the barbs also served as pins for clothes when not holding meat to the line). Hanging the meat like this, which the women did for one or two days, improved the flavor by allowing the enzymes to break down the tissue through dry aging. The evaporation of the meat's water also helped to concentrate the flavor. Later, they would put the meat in boiling water to rehydrate it.

Of course, the women had to keep a watchful eye on the weather—if it began to rain, they would have to snatch the meat off the line to prevent maggots from infesting it and to avoid having to salt it again.

Once the meat was dried, the women would bring it inside and hang it in their kitchen; most colony families had no refrigerators. When they cooked for the day, they would simply grab a slab of meat from where it hung and put it in a pan.

The carcass would not only provide us plenty of good meat; it would also be used to make soap. The men would place the intestines in a wheelbarrow, and the women would push the barrow down to the river, where they would hold the intestines in the running water to be cleansed. The kids—both from the ranch and the colony—would tag along, fascinated by the process, which could take all morning—but you didn't rush it, as you wanted to completely cleanse the intestines.

Once they were clean, the women would put them back in the wheelbarrow, push them up to the colony, and cook them in fifty-five-gallon barrels behind one of the houses, pouring an equal amount of lye into the barrel. The barrels were set on bricks with a large fire going under them, and the women would cook the concoction until it turned to liquid. Kids were not allowed near the barrels because of the potential danger of the barrel tipping and falling, but that wasn't a problem for me: the intestines and lye stank as it was cooking.

I should pause a moment to admit that my harebrained and mischievous brother, Jimmy, would be telling the guests to drink up from the river, *after* we had cleaned the intestines in it. (While the intestines were being cleaned, Jimmy would make sure to have the guests downstream, out of sight of the cleansing.) "It's the purest water in all of Brazil," he would say, and people would smile and cup their hands to drink the river water. Thankfully, to the best of my knowledge, none of our visitors became ill from this.

After the intestines and lye had cooked for about two days, the mixture would be cooled and the women would cut the soap in twelve-inch chunks. Later they would cut pieces off these chunks for household use.

The soap-making process was divvied up among groups of three colony families at a time; each steer would generally provide enough soap for three families for a year.

It's interesting the things most people take for granted. You want meat? Go to the grocery store. Soap? Same thing. You don't need to see the gritty and gruesome processes that produced that meat and soap. You don't have to see the blood drain from a slaughtered animal or smell the stench of its intestines as they are somehow miraculously turned into something that you will willingly rub on your body to—of all things—*cleanse* yourself.

Ranch life is filled with all kinds of eye-opening, jaw-dropping, and sometimes stomach-churning tasks and duties that define a rancher's everyday life.

There's one more thing that people often take for granted, particularly in this Information Age that we live in. We now have instant access to all the news, entertainment, and information that we want—right at our fingertips, just a few keystrokes away.

My time in Brazil, of course, predated the Information Age. Compared to the technology available today, we were living in the Stone Age. And as kids, we were dying for a little fun, a little entertainment.

So, we kids did what every red-blooded child is DNA-programmed to do: we nagged, badgered, bothered, and tormented our parents until they gave in to the idea of purchasing a television for the ranch.

Oh, the excitement! The idea of it was like Christmas 365 days a year! As soon as we had nagged enough that Mom promised a trip into Presidente Prudente to look at TVs, we were little angels. We became polite and helpful almost to the point of our mother suspecting that someone had abducted us and replaced us with carbon copies that looked like us but didn't quite know how to *act* like us. But we were not going to get her riled and take back her promise of looking at TVs.

One glorious summer Saturday morning when I was eleven years old, my mother piled all the kids—Jimmy, Theresa, Michael, and me—into our Rural Willys Wagon. The Rural was one of the most useful vehicles for driving on muddy roads—which we had plenty of—because of its high wheelbase. It looked like a tank, all boxy and solid, and was far from a luxury ride. You could feel every bump in the road, and on particularly rutted roads, a car door would sometimes fly open. I was always terrified of falling out of the car, and instinctively leaned toward the center of the vehicle on bad roads. I'm still nervous about sitting next to a door in a moving car to this day.

Our ranch driver drove us in this boxy contraption to Prudente, two hours away. (We always had a driver for these trips—my mother never drove—and the trip could be a rather adventurous one, with rutted dirt roads that, during the rainy season, from December through March, would flood and be treacherous to navigate. More than once on these trips we had to be pulled out by a tractor; in fact, a tractor was always sent along with us during the rainy season to pull us out of the low areas that didn't drain well. Our car would be splattered with mud by the time we got to Prudente. It wasn't until we reached the town of Pirapozinho—about two-thirds of the way to Prudente—that we had the luxury of paved roads.) As our driver parked on one of the downtown streets in front of an electronics store that was advertising a big sale, we couldn't hold our excitement any longer and began to pester Mom with questions.

"Are we actually taking it home today?" "How big will it be?" "How many stations will we get?" "What shows will be on it?" "Where are we going to put it?" "Can I choose the first show we watch?"

"If you kids don't shut up, you won't get a TV at all!" my mother snapped as she walked briskly into the store. We trailed her like little ducklings, spilling into the store and fanning out to check out all the Colorado, Emerson, and Philco TVs that lined the shelves. Thinking back, they were big, boxy, knobby, and ugly, but to us back then, they were exquisite pearls of exceeding beauty and wonder.

We continued our pestering in the store until we got what we called "the eye" from Mom. That was the dark and foreboding look she gave us that forewarned of a major eruption if we didn't immediately stop whatever we were doing and behave.

"Shut up!" I hissed at Jimmy, who was doing no more badgering than I was. But I wanted to show Mom that as the oldest child I understood, that I would marshal the troops, get them in line.

What I really wanted was to get a TV in our car and get it home.

The salesman, with a nervous eye on us kids, swiftly directed Mom to a Colorado and sold her on all its virtues. Once we knew we were getting that TV, we were elated. It seemed to take forever for Mom to sign a bunch of papers at the counter—just give the man his money and let's get out of here—but two salesmen lugged the heavy box out to our car and put it in the trunk. We couldn't close the trunk lid; we had to tie it down with rope.

Back home, the driver and the houseboy carried the bulky box into the house—it was too heavy for us to lug—and we set it up in the room where our tutor helped us navigate our school correspondence courses (we didn't attend a brick-and-mortar school). Later that day, when Dad came in, I heard Mom and him talking in the living room. At first their voices were calm and normal, but soon there was an edge to Dad's, and his volume rose a notch or two.

"You did *what*?" he said.

"I told you. Just calm down. The salesman said—"

"I know what he said. He told you to buy the TV on time because it would be easier on you to pay a small monthly payment."

"He said it was the normal thing to do for such a large item," she said defensively. "They even sell things like blenders on time."

"Of course they do! You know why? Because then they can about double their profit on everything they sell! Do you know how high their interest rates are?"

"Well, no, but . . . "

My father groaned in frustration. He looked at the papers for the sale and he groaned even louder. He instructed his employees to never buy things on time—the very thing his wife had just done. (I later learned that the military government of Brazil incentivized stores to sell TVs on time, to get them into the hands of people living in the country's interior. The government wanted to get a unified message out to the people, and TVs were often sold at a lower interest rate than other products. The military took over in 1964, and this was a big part of their communications plan.)

We kids, of course, couldn't have cared less what the payment plan was. The TV was in the house, and that meant that we didn't have to go down to the colony to watch in our friends' houses.

Getting a TV, understand, was a much bigger deal to us then than it is now to go down to a box store and plunk some money down on a 65-inch OLED or QLED television. To that point, our only choice to watch TV was to go down to the bookkeeper's house, who kindly invited us to watch with him once in a while. His was the first TV on the ranch. We would sit in his living room and watch a few *novelas*—soap operas—and then go back to our house.

The father of my good friend Zenia bought the second TV on the ranch. Her parents would close the window and shut the curtains so other people couldn't stand outside and watch, but they invited us (and us only) in to watch with them. Social ladders exist everywhere, and they considered themselves at or near the top.

As a few others not quite as high on that social ladder began to purchase TVs, they didn't shut their windows or use curtains to block the view from outside. In fact, they left everything open—and charged a fee for anyone who wanted to stand outside their window and watch TV!

So, yes, we were thrilled to be getting our *own* TV, believe me.

However, the viewing experience was vastly different compared to what it is today.

We didn't have hundreds of channels to choose from (there are currently more than 1,700 commercial stations on the air in the US!). We had one—that's right, *one*—channel. It was on the air from 5 p.m. to 10 p.m. The channel, Rede Global, aired three soap operas and a couple of other shows, and later exported numerous *novelas* to other countries. The black-and-white picture was, well, not quite crystal clear. At times it would get so grainy and snowy that we would tell the houseboy to go out on the roof and adjust the antenna. He would work it this way and that, shouting "How's that?," and when the picture got to its clearest point, we'd shout "Stop! It's good!" We even tried placing translucent plastic screens over the TV to enhance the picture; a blue one seemed to help the picture the best. Once we placed a rainbow-hued screen over the TV and shouted "It's just like grandma's back in Texas—a color TV!"

The maids would come in and watch with us kids at night; they were engrossed in the soaps. My parents just watched a few select events: the Olympics, the World Cup, the moon landing in 1969, Formula 1 races.

Going to Presidente Prudente was always a treat for us, because it was a real city, unlike all the other dusty little towns and villages that we encountered near the ranch. Prudente had an actual skyline, fine dining, and one high-quality hotel where people with real money stayed. I remember our parents going to Prudente for New Year's Eve celebrations; they would stay at the Perete Hotel and go to a nightclub, meeting other ranch managers there to bring in the new year. And about once a month, they would take us kids to stay overnight at the Perete, and we would take turns choosing where we would eat. Jimmy would always choose *churrasco* (barbecue); I would go for Chinese food. The owner of the Chinese restaurant that we frequented got to know us; he was a very friendly and outgoing man. He told us his brother worked on the set of some of John Wayne's movies, and he loved to show us pictures of John Wayne and regale us with colorful stories about the actor.

(A bit less reputable than the finer hotels of Brazil were its motels—and with names like The Endless Love Motel, 24 Hours of Love, You 'n' Me, and so on, you can understand why. People who wanted to experience, ahem, a little "afternoon delight," would pull up to a stall in front of a room of one of these motels, which were typically tucked away down a narrow road. An attendant would pop out and open a cheap garage door so the client could pull in, and the door would be shut so no one could see the car. After the client had conducted his "business" in the room, he would call the front desk, and the attendant would bring the bill and put it on a lazy Susan, swinging the bill into the room. It was all very discreet. I guess you could call it "Love, Brazilian Style.")

We would also do our major grocery shopping in Prudente, getting items that we couldn't find in the villages around us; we would do such shopping about once a month. Our driver would get the grocery items while Mom would go in for massages or to have her hair done. I took piano lessons in Prudente—quite the trip to learn an instrument! All of these trips would be full-day excursions, and they were always anticipated with excitement.

I guess I should amend that: going to Prudente was *almost* always a treat for us. The one bad thing about Prudente is that's where our dentist, Dr. Nogueira, practiced. I'm sure in Jimmy's mind he hadn't practiced enough, because unless Dr. Nogueira's goal was to produce unremitting fear and pain in his patients, he was not very good.

Dr. Nogueira didn't believe in using novocaine, for mysterious and perhaps sadistic reasons. I would be called in first, as the oldest child; Jimmy would be sweating bullets in the waiting room, huffing and puffing while he awaited his turn in the torture chamber.

In Dr. Nogueira's office was a picture of two men sitting at a table. One guy was smiling and eating corn on the cob with an obviously healthy set of teeth; the other guy was toothless, sad, and sipping soup. (My dad would joke with Theresa, who had the worst teeth in the family, that she was going to end up like that toothless soup-sipper someday.)

As you sat in the patient's chair, you had a closeup view—way *too* close, for Jimmy's tastes—of various drill bits that Dr. Nogueira used to carry out his torture with. Some of those bits looked big enough to use on an elephant, though they might have grown a bit in my memory. Still, I do remember sitting there sweating and wondering if he was going to have to use any of those bits on me—and hoping for the smallest one, if so.

Once I was finished, he would call Jimmy in. Jimmy would cry and scream and beg for mercy, and the dentist and an assistant would have to cajole and push and drag him into the office and do everything short of strapping him into the chair. I honestly think Jimmy—and everyone else in the office, including Dr. Noguiera—would have been happier if

Dr. Noguiera had just punched him out and worked on him while he was in la-la land.

Mom couldn't stand all the yelling and screaming, so she would have the driver drop us off at the dentist's and she would go shopping elsewhere. When she came to the office after her shopping, she'd pay the bill and ask Dr. Noguiera how it went.

"The Italian, he give me trouble, as usual," Dr. Noguiera bemoaned. He called Jimmy "the Italian" because he said all Italians were cowards. "He cried and screamed, and one time he tried to bite me."

"Almost got him, too," Jimmy muttered to me.

"Well, he's young," my mother said, trying to hold back a smile. It seemed clear to me that she thought Dr. Noguiera probably deserved to be bitten. "He's a bit scared of you."

"Scared of me?" Dr. Noguiera said, wide-eyed. "It's me who is scared of *him*. Every time he comes in here, it's a wrestling match to get him in the chair, and a wrestling match to keep him in it."

Out of pity for us kids and especially for Jimmy, Mom would have the driver take us to get ice cream after our trips to the dentist. I think it was the only way she could coerce Jimmy to get in the car to go to Prudente.

And then there were the overnight trips to São Paulo. We loved going on these trips, which my dad would need to take for business meetings. He was kind enough to take the whole family along, knowing how much fun it would be for us kids to see the big city—and it was truly *big*; its metro area population was over 7 million at the time. It seems funny to me now that we didn't want to leave our luxurious hotel in São Paulo, the Cambridge Hotel, to explore the wonders of the city (with adults, of course)—but Mom was always afraid the maids, who came along with us, would get lost, or be run over on the busy streets. That was totally fine with us, because the TV in our hotel room had much better reception than ours at home, and got more channels.

Those trips were a big deal for our maids, too. They had never been to a city larger than the tiny towns and villages surrounding the ranch. They walked around with huge eyes the whole time we would stay in São Paulo. The Cambridge was a high-rise, which scared them to death, because they had likely never been higher than two stories off the ground.

The rooms we stayed in were huge, with ceiling-to-floor velvet curtains, which I loved, though a friend of Mom's once said it made her feel like she was in a coffin. We got a kick out of ordering room service—we kids would fight over who would push the button for the service. We preferred eating in our room because it was fun to order the food to be sent up.

We would, on occasion, give up watching TV (*The Beverly Hillbillies, Bonanza,* and cartoons, all dubbed in Portuguese) to explore parts of the city near the Cambridge. My favorite place to go was Mappin, a huge department store with origins in England. The store was the driving force in Brazil behind the installment plan (no doubt to my father's disgust), and for many years was where the elite met and shopped. It had *everything* in it; you could wander up and down its aisles and sections for hours and never get bored. (Well, my father couldn't, but I could.)

That's the way life was growing up on a ranch in Brazil. Times of boredom and tedium were interspersed with times of excitement and joy. We certainly became masters at manufacturing our own fun, whether we were on the ranch by ourselves, or with the colony kids or with our family or entertaining ranch guests, or in Presidente Prudente or São Paulo. All of it was a rich and varied learning experience, no matter which ranch we were living on, no matter which colony kids became our friends. In fact, looking back, moving around the different ranches made it all the more interesting—though I didn't always like the move at the time—and helped teach me some valuable life lessons.

CHAPTER 5

RANCHERS, FRIENDS, AND OTHER ODDBALLS

MY MOTHER LOVED TO RECOUNT THE STORY of my encounter with a spider monkey at Laranja Doce when I was a mere one-year-old.

The monkey came courtesy of Carson and Ellen Geld, who quickly became my parents' best friends in Brazil.

"Oh good Lord," my mother told me decades later. "You never knew what to expect when the Gelds came over. You had to be prepared for *anything*."

The Gelds, like my parents, were expatriates from the US; they came from Mansfield, Ohio, to live in Presidente Prudente and work for Anderson, Clayton, and Company, a Houston-based corporation that is the world's largest trader of cotton and other agricultural commodities. Carson and Ellen had moved to Brazil to set up a sustainable agricultural model through Anderson Clayton, which Ellen's father had developed in Ohio. My parents met Carson and Ellen soon after the Gelds moved to Brazil.

The Gelds thought it would be a grand idea on their initial visit to our ranch in Laranja Doce to bring their two boxers, one as homely looking as the next, along with Chico, their spider monkey. Chico was a quite cute and intelligent-looking creature with dark brown arms, back, and head, and tannish-gray whiskers and chest.

As a one-year-old, my only expectation for the evening was to sit in a high chair and be fed banana mush by one of our maids. The four adults,

Elizabeth (Betinha), 1960. Author collection.

meanwhile, talked and laughed it up over cocktails as they shared stories about adjusting to a new country and a new culture and a whole new way of life in this country far south of the US border. My mother no doubt was holding court, in her element as the center of attention and chief storyteller. She and Ellen hit it off immediately and became lifelong friends.

The social merriment was cut short, however, by a maid and a baby who were shrieking in tandem at rather high volume in the kitchen.

"It sounded like the roof had caved in!" my mother said later. In the moment, she ran into the kitchen and immediately joined in on the shrieking, all of which was for Chico, who in his exploration of the house had been drawn to the kitchen, where he smelled the banana mush I was being fed. Having watched the maid spoon the mush into my mouth several times and realizing the maid had no intention of spooning *him* mush anytime soon, the brazen creature hopped onto my high chair tray, quick as a wink climbed onto my head, and leaned over to take the glass jar of banana mush from where the maid had dropped it on my high chair tray. He then began using his finger to scoop out a snack for himself. The maid, wild-eyed, was trying to shoo the monkey away from my head without actually being brave enough to touch it; I, just as wild-eyed, screamed bloody murder; and my mother, who nearly slammed the swinging door off its hinges as she tore into the kitchen, shrieked the loudest of all, perhaps not wanting to be outdone by a maid and an infant.

As Ellen and Carson Geld and my father traipsed into the kitchen, Chico by this time either had his fill of the banana mush or of these loudmouthed screaming humans, and he hopped onto the tray, then onto the floor, and scurried away to find a little peace and quiet. In the meantime, Ellen had rushed over, laughing all the while, to assure my mom that all was okay, while the men doubled over in laughter. The maid, meanwhile, was fanning herself with her hand to cool down and was saying over and over to herself, but loudly enough for all to hear, "Não há macacos na cozinha! Não há macacos na cozinha!" ("No monkeys in the kitchen!")

Carson Geld quit working for Anderson Clayton, in 1961, and he and Ellen purchased a small farm in Tietê, about two hours west of São Paulo. They raised five children in Brazil; as I grew to be a toddler and older, I spent long afternoons playing with the Geld children. I remember Carson would call his kids over when he was milking cows; he would tell them to open their mouths, and he would try to squirt some milk into their mouths. He was consistent: he always missed. The kids would laugh and scream at him, with milk running down their necks and soaking their shirts. Carson was also in the habit of naming his cows: Bessie, Maude, Eileen. We thought it was funny. We'd tell Dad this, and add that we wanted to name our calves, but he'd shake his head and say, "The animals are not to have names. We might be eating that calf for dinner at some point. No names!" Real ranchers, I learned, did not name their animals. But Carson marched to the beat of a different drummer, and he went on naming his cows and drenching his kids with milk.

And then there was the time, many years later, that Carson and Ellen drove me and some of their children home from boarding school in Campinas, about eight hours away from our ranch. It happened to be their oldest daughter's birthday; they were determined to have a party for Robin, even though it was pouring rain. So they pulled under a bridge in Avaré, about halfway home, to have a little party, but it was still raining, and the mud on the side of the narrow road was thick and gooey, so Carson got the bright idea that we all should crawl onto the roof of the station wagon, sing happy birthday, and eat Robin's cake. We were partially protected from the rain, but still ended up getting soaked, laughing and screaming as we ate the cake. We didn't finish it, so Carson ran the cake over to a family living in a nearby shack. He pounded on the door and a woman opened it, looking at this madman who was holding half a cake in his hands and talking in some strange language to her, the rain pouring off of his hat and down his back. She looked a bit frightened at first, then bewildered; finally, she smiled and took the remains of the cake from the babbling man, who then turned and jogged back to a carful of laughing people.

This was, of course, something my parents would *never* do—in fact, pretty much anything Carson did, my dad would never do—yet they became fast friends, in part because Carson was as loveable and good-natured as he was zany. Certainly there was never a dull moment around the Gelds.

So, yes, the Gelds thought and lived differently from most people, and that's why it didn't seem strange to them to bring a monkey into someone's house on their initial visit. They lived a bit of a bohemian lifestyle; they would have been just at home in the '60s in Haight-Ashbury as they were on a farm in southeastern Brazil. Ellen wrote multiple books, including one titled *View from the Fazenda: A Tale of the Brazilian Heartlands.* When I bought the book from her in the early 2000s, as she signed a copy for me, we reminisced about our families' times together in Brazil. "Ah, I remember you, of course! I will always think of you as the one with the monkey perched on her head."

Yes, that was me: the little girl with the monkey on her head. Perhaps minimally better than having a monkey on one's back, though I didn't think so at the time.

Ellen Geld came by her writing (and her farming) honestly. Her father, Louis Bromfield, wrote more than three dozen books and won the Pulitzer Prize in 1927 for his novel *Early Autumn.* He wrote bestsellers throughout the 1920s and '30s, and also worked briefly in Hollywood as a contract screenwriter for Samuel Goldwyn, Jr.

He was part of the expatriate community of American writers in Paris during the 1920s and '30s. He counted among his Parisian literary friends Ernest Hemingway, Edith Wharton, Sinclair Lewis, and Gertrude Stein. He brought his family back to the States when World War II was looming in Europe, buying 581 acres near Mansfield, Ohio, and becoming an early proponent of organic and self-sustaining gardening. Bromfield developed a technique known as conservation farming, based on grass farming. It was this approach that served as a model for sustainable agriculture. His farm, Malabar Farm, was one of the first to stop using pesticides; today, thousands of visitors flock annually to Malabar Farm State Park (the farm, facing foreclosure, was deeded to the state and became a state park in 1976). Bromfield served as best man at the Malabar Farm wedding of Humphrey Bogart and Lauren Bacall. The farm attracted writers, film stars, politicians, and conservationists from across the nation.

The Renwicks—Duncan and Margaret, along with their redheaded kids, Heather (the same age as me), Karleen (one year younger), and Andrew (six years younger)—also became great family friends. They were Scottish, and spoke in thick Scottish accents; Duncan was a thin, spry man who liked to smoke a pipe and appear erudite. They always—*always*—had their "spot of tea" in the afternoon; a monsoon rain could be lashing against their house, threatening to carry the house away in a flash flood, and Margaret might say, "Do you think we should gather the children and try to find higher ground, dear?," to which Duncan would no doubt reply, "Well, certainly not until we've had our spot of tea, darling."

Margaret fascinated me, because nothing ever ruffled her. When all hell was breaking loose—which it often would when the Renwicks came to visit—Margaret would calmly observe the chaos or damage and make comments like "Oh well," or "That's not so bad, now, is it?" My mother, of course, was on the other extreme: to her, of *course* it was bad!

The Renwicks lived on Mosquito Ranch while we were at Laranja Doce. Duncan was a fun-loving and rather quirky character; if there were a fire in the kitchen, he might respond with, "Oh, well. I hope they can get it out without anyone being hurt. Now, what were you saying?" I remember one time he threw a costume party and appeared wrapped in an animal skin and making strange grunting and hooting noises. Another man—certainly not my father!—dressed in a maid's uniform for the occasion. These parties would be attended by the families of all five ranches, including a Swedish couple who ran Formosa Ranch. Formosa was my favorite ranch; its tall eucalyptus groves and crystal-clear dams made it seem like a picturesque paradise to me. When these parties were held at Mosquito Ranch (before we lived there), we had to endure a two-hour drive on a winding, bumpy, and sometimes treacherously muddy dirt road, but it was always worth it.

Because of the distance involved, these were overnight soirées—which we kids loved. We would arrive in time for a huge barbecue luncheon, after which the adults would break away to either talk or take a little siesta while the kids would run off to play. The nights were always filled with music, dancing, card playing, a bit of drinking, and a lot of laughter.

It was just as fun for us kids, because we would have a cowboy chaperone who would organize horseback rides for us, and with our maids we would have mini picnics on the banks of the Paranapanema River.

Heather and Karleen Renwick and I would have great fun together doing the types of goofy things that kids do: traipsing around the house wrapped in bedspreads as ultra-cool princesses; pretending we were Braniff flight attendants (who dressed quite stylishly); sequestering ourselves in the guest house on Mosquito Ranch and making believe we were sipping "adult drinks" and having "adult conversations" (which, around our house and around the rest of the ranches, at least during these get-togethers, often bordered on the insane); or forming what we called our "caterpillar band." (The genius behind that name escapes me now.) Our instruments were pots and pans, our songs were all our own, and we proudly taped the clanging racket to play it for all the adults so they could enjoy our "concert." Poor Jimmy, two years younger than me, would constantly pester us girls to be part of the band. At this stage of his life, pestering was one of his primary talents, and though we loathed having a boy join our band, we finally acquiesced, telling him he could blow his stupid cattle horn while we banged on our pots and pans and recorded the piece for the parents. Ecstatic, he joined in, blowing at odd intervals while we girls clanged and banged away, making what we assumed was a joyous noise. Jimmy was so happy to be part of the band that he actually thanked us after the song was over and asked if we were going to play it for the parents. He couldn't wait to tell them all that he was the one blowing the horn, which sounded like a sick cow bellowing for help.

Later that evening, when we played for the adults the song that we had taped *before* Jimmy came along, we three girls almost fell over laughing once Jimmy realized his horn had not been recorded. He threw a fit and ran out of the living room, and Mom seized the opportunity to tell us girls to go after him and apologize. It didn't dawn on me until years later that she was simply shooing us away so the adults would not have to listen to any more of that horrendous clattering that we had so kindly recorded for them.

Betinha, Mary Lee, Theresa, Michael, Jimmy, 1964. Author collection.

As Jimmy, Theresa, and Michael—I was the oldest, and all four of us siblings were two years apart—got to be of school age, that presented a dilemma for our parents. We were homeschooled to begin with, but while our mother was trained as a teacher, that was as a high school teacher. The homeschooling would work through eighth grade, but beyond that, we needed another solution.

Many of the Brazilian ranch owners would rent a house in town for the mother and children to live in during the week, and the kids would go to school in town before returning with their mother to the ranch for weekends and holidays. The English families living in Brazil would often send their kids back to England for boarding school, leaving in September and returning in May. The Renwicks sent their kids back to the UK for boarding school starting with first grade.

Our parents chose neither of those options and had numerous discussions about the school issue, some of them more heated than others.

Looking back, if there was ever a logical time for us to return as a family to Texas, it would have been when we were in our elementary school years. Dad even brought that up a time or two, but Mom would have nothing of it. She was adamant about staying in Brazil. She was, obviously, still reveling in her Queen Bee status in her new country.

It so happened that Francis Herbert, president of the operations and Dad's boss, was visiting my parents one evening not long after Mom and Dad had had another of their "conversations" about our schooling. Francis visited the ranches several times a year, and was a congenial and affable man in his thirties.

After dinner, Mom served Dad and Francis glasses of bourbon on the large patio outside. It was in the fall, still quite pleasant out; crickets and cicadas were chirping their evening songs, and the night sky was full of brilliant stars. Francis thanked Mom for the drink and then gazed up at the sky.

"This is something you don't see in São Paulo," he said.

"The stars are amazing out here, aren't they?" Mom said.

They sipped their drinks and chatted, and in relatively short order, Mom brought out the bottle of bourbon and poured fresh drinks.

"Oh, I shouldn't," Francis said, but Mom convinced him one more drink wouldn't hurt, so he took it, and they continued chatting. Eventually, Mom casually turned the conversation to the topic of homeschooling.

"It's so hard to do, with four kids and all," Mom said, sipping her drink.

"I'll bet it is," Francis agreed.

Dad scowled but said nothing.

"And there's so much to do on the ranch," Mom added. "I guess if I had nothing else to do, it wouldn't be so hard, but as you can imagine . . ."

"Oh, for sure. I'm sure you're busy as a bee," Francis said, slurring his words just slightly.

"We're doing okay," Dad grumbled, but no one appeared to hear him.

"And the kids' education—well, what's more important than that?" Mom said.

"They need a top-notch education, no doubt about it," Francis agreed. "You need it nowadays to get ahead, to get a good job."

"Of course you do," Mom said. She could see that she was pushing Dad's buttons a bit much, so she slacked off a bit, turning the conversation to Francis, asking if he had found a girl yet, or was dating a bevy of them. "You must be one of the most eligible bachelors in São Paulo," she said.

"Oh, I'm hardly that," Francis said, blushing.

Dad rolled his eyes and excused himself to go to the bathroom.

"Francis," Mom said after Dad was out of earshot, "don't you think it would be a good idea if the company hired a tutor? To help with the schooling on the ranch?"

"A tutor? Well, I don't know . . . "

"Think of it! It would pay off, because the ranch would run more smoothly—please don't tell me you're the old-fashioned type who thinks the only work done on a ranch is by a *man*. . . "

"Oh, no, of course not!" Francis said, waving his arm in objection. "I'd never—"

"Here, let me freshen your drink." Mom poured a bit more bourbon into his glass.

"I don't know if I should have more . . . "

"Nonsense! I'm just freshening it. So anyway, having a tutor on the ranch would help me out, free me up to make sure all the operations run smoothly—Pete would be at a loss without my organizational skills—and the kids would benefit by not falling behind in their studies and being ready by the time it's ready for boarding school."

"Ah, I see," Francis said, swirling his bourbon a bit and taking another sip. "This bourbon really is amazing."

"You know what, Francis? I think I agree with you. Yes, yes I do. That's a wonderful idea."

"Agree with . . . what? What's a wunnerful idea?" His speech was slipping further; apparently, he was not a big drinker.

"Why, to hire a tutor for the ranch! It's brilliant, actually!"

"Yes, but . . . is it? Did I say . . . ?"

Mom reached over and patted his arm. "Oh, Francis, you are always so modest! It's no wonder you have all those city girls fawning all over you!"

She began laughing, and Francis joined in, no doubt unsure as to what they were laughing about. But, as Dad returned, it sounded like Mom and Francis were lifelong friends sharing an inside joke.

"Pete!" she said as he returned to his chair. "I have wonderful news! Francis, should you tell him, or should I?"

"Umm . . . you go ahead."

"Very well. Francis just informed me that the company wants to hire a tutor for the ranch."

Dad furrowed his brow and looked at Francis. "Is that so?"

"Well, uh . . . "

"He thought it would be best for the kids, and he knows how important their education is," Mom said. "He was concerned about them falling behind, what with all my other duties on the ranch."

"Is that right, Francis?" Dad said.

Francis thought about it a moment, then nodded his head vigorously. "Yes, absolutely! It's really past time we did something like this. I don't know why I hadn't thought of it before," Francis said.

"I'm just glad you thought of it now," Mom said, smiling demurely at him.

Dad took a deep breath and slowly exhaled. He saw how those bright stars above them had aligned, once he'd gone inside.

"Yeah, perfect," he said, giving Mom a knowing look. She beamed back at him and then gazed back up at the stars.

"So, you don't see a night sky like this in São Paulo, do you, Francis?" she said.

"Oh, no," he said. "Not in a million years."

A few weeks later, a thick battle-ax who looked like a cross between a bloated Wicked Witch of the West and the Grim Reaper showed up on our doorstep at Mosquito Ranch. Wasting no energy on smiling, she introduced herself to my mother as "Mrs. Murray, hired to be a tutor to your children" in a gravelly, no-nonsense voice. (Francis had called my mom several days earlier, saying that a tutor was heading our way.) I hid behind Mom, afraid the lady might snatch me up and fly me away on her broom.

"And who is this?" she stated more than asked, nodding at the trembling little girl hiding behind her mother's skirt.

Mom, putting her arm around my shoulder and bringing me gently forward, said, "This is my oldest child, Betinha. Betinha, can you say hi to Mrs. Murray?"

I attempted to speak, but nothing got past the giant lump of fear and loathing in my throat. Something about this woman, who was nearly as wide as she was tall, brought about a deep mistrust in me, something akin to the American-Soviet Union relationship of the early '60s. I was entering Day 1 of the Emmert children's Cold War with Mrs. Murray.

"Humph," Mrs. Murray said. "It appears someone needs to be taught some manners."

Even my mother, who feared no one, seemed oddly taken aback by this Menace from Maryland and unsure of how to respond to her brusque manner of communicating.

"She's just . . . a little shy at the moment," my mother finally said. Which was far from the truth. Intimidated, frightened, appalled, yes. Shy, no.

"You have four children, do you not?" Mrs. Murray said in more of an accusation than a question.

"I do," my mother admitted, sounding as if she were responding to a prosecuting attorney's question.

"Well?" Mrs. Murray said.

My mother stared blankly at this dark storm that stood just inside our doorway—was it too late to push her out the door, slam it shut, and lock it?—until she realized Mrs. Murray wanted to inspect the full troops.

Never had I seen my mother so obeisant before. She dutifully rounded up Jimmy, who was more interested in dislodging a booger from his nose (I would have paid all the money in my piggy bank to see him dislodge said booger and then shake hands with Mrs. Murray, but alas, that was a fantasy unfulfilled), Theresa, and Michael, until all four of us kids were staring dolefully at this woman who was for some reason being inflicted on us. I think we would have unanimously voted for Mom to continue teaching us on her own, or, barring that, for us to enter some juvenile detention facility, rather than be subject to the rule of Mrs. Murray. But we did not get to vote.

"Children, this is Mrs. Murray," Mom said, regaining a bit of her Queen Bee status as the interrogation went on. "She's going to be your tutor."

"What's a tutor?" Jimmy asked, wiping the picked booger on his pants.

"A tutor is someone who is going to help me teach you kids. She'll be like a teacher, helping you with your school subjects. She will be tutoring Theresa and Michael; I'll still be teaching you and Betinha." I was eight at the time; Jimmy was six.

A look of relief materialized on Jimmy's face. Theresa stayed silent but scowled. Little Michael simply burst into tears and ran off wailing.

Thus, Mrs. Murray was ushered into our lives, like it or not.

Sometimes first impressions turn out to be wrong. I only wish this were true in the case of Mrs. Murray. But no, we had pegged her for the miserable hag that she was.

We learned that Mrs. Murray, her husband, and their son Gary had come from Maryland to Brazil a few years earlier. The Murrays had purchased a small farm outside of São Paulo and were keeping bees and living off the land. But soon enough their bees were attacked by African bees, also known as killer bees, having killed over one thousand people as well as innumerable horses and other animals. These bees tend to sting relentlessly, ten times more than honey bees, and Mrs. Murray was stung so many times in trying to defend her own bees that she came close to dying. We learned it would take more than a swarm of angry killer bees to bring down Mrs. Murray. We also learned that Mr. and Mrs. Murray were either separated or divorced, and Gary lived with his father in São Paulo. And we further discovered that the Murrays had *driven* all the way from Maryland to Brazil, which probably took a few months. Most of the trip would have been on two-lane highways, including many dirt and gravel roads in Central and South America. We couldn't blame Mr. Murray for being separated from his wife not long after they settled in Brazil.

But here Mrs. Murray was, inside our door, ready to unleash her full fury on us. Making matters infinitely worse was that Mrs. Murray was to live with us. As in the best of horror movies, the evil was in the house and there was no escaping. She took over an unused bedroom, we converted the TV room to a schoolroom, and our life with Mrs. Murray began.

Of course, I am exaggerating; she was not evil, and she was not . . . well, actually, she *was* all those other things. But she had a good side to her as well.

For instance, she loved crafts, as did I, and we did a lot of finger painting and coloring and crafting little crafty things and piano playing, though the piano was not quite fit for Carnegie Hall. It had been left at Laranja Doce by an Englishman who had lived on the ranch; some of the ivory keys were peeling off, and the piano proved nearly impossible to tune (and completely impossible to stay in tune for more than a day or so).

Even so, Mrs. Murray was simply one of those people who begged to be tricked, irritated, antagonized, and provoked. Which we kids took to with a happy vengeance.

For example, I took to playing the same song—"Pica-pau" ("Woodpecker") over and over, to the rising irritation of Mrs. Murray, who thought the first ten renditions or so was plenty of music about woodpeckers. (I was taking piano lessons in Presidente Prudente, and the truth is, I hated the instrument and I hated practicing, but it *was* a tool with which I could torture Mrs. Murray. So it had that going for it.)

"Do you not know any other songs, child?" Mrs. Murray would say, exasperated. She had been working with the other three kids and my playing had rattled her enough that she had just knocked over a jar of glue.

"No ma'am," I would say innocently, and then start the next rendition. I was stopped only when Mrs. Murray would come over and slam the wooden keyboard cover over the keys. She was never quite quick enough to catch my fingers with the cover. I thought it was a fun game.

"This child has no desire to learn the piano! And no discernible talent for doing so!" she finally barked at my mother.

"She will continue to practice," Mom said, having fully regained her Queen Bee persona. No one was going to tell *her* whether her child could play the piano or not.

Mrs. Murray grumbled under her breath as she walked away, and gave me the evil eye when she saw me sitting on the piano bench, smiling demurely at her.

In my mind, I saw her change into the Wicked Witch of the West, saying *I'll get you, my pretty, and your little dog too!*

From then on, whenever I practiced, Mrs. Murray would find reason to leave the room. Which took all the fun out of practicing for me.

We were not limited to playing pranks on Mrs. Murray indoors; we had the great outdoors to work with, too. But there was one time when the fun and games (for us) crossed over into a bit of a scare.

It all started with Mrs. Murray floating in our pool. She didn't know how to swim, but her buoyant body allowed her to float quite nicely. Typically she floated on her back, but for some reason, once in a while she turned over and floated face down.

One summer afternoon as she was floating on her back, a thunderstorm was fast approaching. The skies were darkening, and we could hear low rumbles of thunder in the distance.

The storm came up quicker than we thought, but Mrs. Murray stayed in the pool as we kids ran around it, playing and getting excited as kids do when a good storm is approaching. Suddenly we heard a loud crack of thunder and saw a flash of lightning very close by. We shrieked and I turned to see Mrs. Murray floating face down in the water, not moving. The lightning had cracked a nearby tree in half and shattered a few windows of our house. As we scurried toward the house, I shouted to my sister and brothers that Mrs. Murray had been struck by lightning and was floating, dead, in our pool!

I wasn't certain that was the case—but then why wasn't she moving? Why didn't she get out of the water? I was half joking when I said that about her being dead, but then I thought maybe she really *was* dead. Maybe we should have gotten her out of the water, warned her about the storm, before it hit. Maybe *we* had caused her death. And *I,* as the oldest, would be the one to blame.

We tore inside our house, screaming for Mom, who came running up, asking what was wrong.

"Mrs. Murray! She's dead! She was hit by lightning and is floating, dead, in our pool!" I spluttered. "I think we *killed* her!" I shrieked.

Mom's look of concern turned to one of bemusement; she was facing the door we had just rushed through from the pool.

I turned around and saw Mrs. Murray coming inside, toweling off her hair, grumbling about the rain.

"Don't touch her!" Jimmy shouted to Michael.

"Why?" Michael asked, not that it was likely he wanted to touch her.

"She's been electrocuted! She'll shock you!"

Mrs. Murray rolled her eyes while Mom laughed.

"I'm not an eel," Mrs. Murray said.

"You . . . you weren't struck by lightning?" I asked.

"Do I look like I was?" she replied.

As I was formulating a response, she made a sudden loud buzzing noise and shot her arm toward me, like she was going to grab me.

Which sent all us kids shrieking one more time, running through the house, anywhere where Mrs. Murray was not present.

A bored kid can quickly turn into a creative and inventive kid, particularly if Mrs. Murray was around to pull a prank on. One day we four kids were walking with Mrs. Murray through a pasture near our house; we were searching for rocks, which Mrs. Murray was fascinated by, near a stream that was just beyond the pasture. Suddenly, several nearby calves, likely just as bored as we were and wanting to investigate these bipeds walking in their pasture, began loping toward us. Mrs. Murray's eyes grew big and her mouth dropped open.

I knew what she was thinking: *we are being stampeded! We are in great danger!*

I winked at the others and then shouted, "Mrs. Murray! Run! They're coming after us!"

"They're going to kill us!" Jimmy gleefully screamed. Theresa and Michael joined in the merriment, screaming and shouting, doing their best not to laugh and give it away.

That was all Mrs. Murray needed. She moved her stout legs faster than I'd ever seen them move, huffing and puffing as she hustled to the barbed wire fence, on the other side of which was safety. When she got to the fence, she lifted a strand of barbed wire so she could slip through, but still managed to cut her leg in the process. Back inside the house, as she cleaned and bandaged her wound, she told my dad what had happened, how we had barely managed to escape harm from those "rampaging beasts out there."

My dad, looking out the window and seeing the calves standing motionless in the pasture, pointed at them and said, "You mean those calves?"

Mrs. Murray nodded. "They were charging us! I hustled the kids away but got cut in the process."

I could see my dad straining to suppress a grin. "Mrs. Murray," he said as kindly as he could, "if you had stopped running, they would have stopped chasing you. They were simply curious."

"But . . . but the kids . . . they said . . . " She narrowed her eyes and glared at me. "You told me they were coming after us!"

Innocently batting my eyelashes, I said, "Well, gosh, Mrs. Murray, it sure *seemed* like they were charging us. Didn't it, Jimmy?"

Jimmy gave an exaggerated nod. "Uh huh. I thought we were goners."

Dad gave us both the eye, but said nothing to us in front of Mrs. Murray.

"You see what I have to put up with?" Mrs. Murray said to my father. "These children are impossible! They have no manners, no respect for their elders!" Turning to us kids, she said, "You should be ashamed of yourselves!" And then she stomped off.

The truth was, we felt pretty good about ourselves. We had turned a boring day into a rather fun one.

The oldest child often has a few advantages over younger siblings. The primary advantage I had as oldest child was I did not have to be taught by Mrs. Murray. And, as mentioned, Jimmy was also still taught by Mom. But Mrs. Murray still seized opportunities to inflict her will on Jimmy and me as well.

For example, she was hired to instill table manners in all four of us. Or rather, she took that responsibility on herself when she saw how lacking we apparently were. In her eyes, we slouched, we passed food incorrectly, we bickered, and we had the general manners of a family of orangutans.

"Mrs. Emmert, I want to teach your children how to behave at a table," she said early on in her stay with us. She must have nearly bit through her tongue to stop from calling us *heathens* or something worse.

"Be my guest," Mom said, to my dismay.

So we suffered through many a dinner with Mrs. Murray conducting us as if were an out-of-synch orchestra—"Jimmy, remember to say *please* and *thank you!*" "Michael, hold your fork this way!" "Theresa, must you *always* have your elbows on the table?" "Betinha, try chewing with your mouth *closed* for once!"

We, of course, continued those bad manners, and more like them, precisely because we knew they would gall Mrs. Murray.

One evening at the dinner table, Mrs. Murray's litany of reproofs regarding our table manners was broken up by a loud thumping on the roof. Aniba, our houseboy who was serving us at the meal, excitedly said, "It is your father! He is up on the roof chasing a possum!"

We all shouted in excitement and asked Mrs. Murray to excuse us from the table—she should have been impressed that we *asked*—but as we pushed back our chairs, she commanded us to stay seated.

"But Mrs. Murray," I began.

"Hush, child! Sit."

We all dolefully sat, and Jimmy, glowering, perched both his elbows on the table, refusing to move them even at the behest of Mrs. Murray, whose frown was so heavy I thought it might collapse the table.

"Jimmy, if you don't remove your elbows from the table at once, I'll—"

We never got to hear the end of the threat, because a nearby rifle shot was echoing in our ears.

That did it. Nothing was going to keep us in our seats—not even Mrs. Murray or her dire threats. We ran outside, Mrs. Murray's rants growing fainter as we shot out the door, and looked up toward the roof, where Dad was hoisting a dead possum by its long, skinny tail. We all cheered. When I turned back toward the house, I saw Mrs. Murray standing just outside the door, hands on her hips, glaring at us.

Later that evening, we heard Mrs. Murray crying in her bedroom. Mom frowned at us and pointed a finger at me because, as the oldest, I was the ringleader. "You kids need to stop pestering her!" she said as she walked down the hall to comfort the poor lady.

I snuck down the hallway and could hear them behind the closed door.

"I can't take any more of this!" Mrs. Murray wailed.

"I've told them to back off," Mom said. She tried to console her, but Mrs. Murray said she'd had enough.

"I'm quitting!" she said. "They don't listen to me! They don't obey me! They just ignore me—or worse, they do the opposite of what I tell them to do! And their father! He's a madman with a gun!"

Mom managed to talk her out of quitting. I actually began to feel guilty, because Mrs. Murray wasn't entirely bad. I did enjoy doing the crafts with her, and she was a decent tutor. I learned a lot from her. I just didn't realize it until much later in life.

Mrs. Murray was simply not made to live on a ranch. She didn't understand life on a ranch, she didn't appreciate the type of people who worked ranches, and she didn't know the language. Which, of course, made it easy to make fun of her while speaking Portuguese.

She also didn't understand certain veterinary techniques, one of which she happened to come across as Jimmy was showing us girls how the vet had performed a rectal palpation on a cow. In what would be understood as an extremely sexist attitude now, girls were not privy to such "intimate" veterinarian maneuvers, though it was fine for boys to watch the procedures.

So, Jimmy used Petisco, one of our oldest and calmest horses, to show us girls just how the vet did the palpation. He had Petisco up against a fence, with a board in front of the horse so he couldn't move. Theresa, her feet perched on one of the wooden fence's slats, lifted Petisco's tail so Jimmy had clear access to the horse's anus, through which he extended his arm.

Just as he had achieved full extension, Mrs. Murray, who had been looking for us, undoubtedly to torture us with more schooling, got schooled herself in the art of rectal palpation.

"Oh my good Lord! Jimmy! Get your hand out of that horse's—get your hand out of there!" Mrs. Murray screeched, causing Jimmy to yank his arm out, Theresa to fall off the fence, and Petisco to knock over the board and bolt away.

"You hose yourself off and then you get inside and take a bath!" Mrs. Murray scolded. "What in the world is *wrong* with you children?"

We tried to explain that was a normal procedure that veterinarians performed on cows and horses for artificial insemination and other medical issues, but she would have none of that. She probably thought we were some sort of strange sexual deviants.

Again, Mrs. Murray quit. Again, my mother talked her into staying. Again, my dad—when Mrs. Murray wasn't around—got a big kick out of the whole thing.

In fact, he never could watch an artificial insemination procedure without a big smile on his face as he thought of Jimmy, Petisco, and Mrs. Murray.

I mentioned Mrs. Murray loved arts and crafts. Under Mrs. Murray's tutelage, we studied the murals of Diego Rivera (whose full name, Diego María de la Concepción Juan Nepomuceno Estanislao de la Rivera y Barrientos Acosta y Rodríguez, we mercifully never had to recite). Rivera was a masterful painter who helped establish the Mexican mural movement in the first half of the twentieth century; he painted murals in Mexico City, Chapingo, Cuernavaca, San Francisco, Detroit, New York City, and many other places.

Duly inspired by the great artist's work, Jimmy, Theresa, and I—Michael was still too young to be dragged into a life of vandalistic crime—decided to honor Rivera, and Mrs. Murray, by rubbing a multitude of various colors of hibiscus flowers on the back wall of our white stucco house. We thought the resulting mural—of our family dogs, Sunset, Sky, and River—was quite stunning.

Mrs. Murray was not with us at the time or she surely would have put a halt to our evolving artistic talents. When we called out our mother to witness our handiwork, she was not as favorably impressed as we imagined she would be. In fact, she expressed her appreciation for our creation by spanking us. Scrubbing the wall had no effect on our mural; workers eventually had to paint over it.

Such is the life of the artist: rarely understood or appreciated.

Mrs. Murray, aided by my mother, would teach us from a curriculum that my parents purchased from Calvert School, an independent school in Baltimore, Maryland. Calvert's homeschooling division, begun in 1905, is considered to be the first of its kind; homeschooling didn't even become legal in all fifty US states until 1993, though the movement for it began in earnest in the 1970s. We would start school at 8:00 a.m., have a snack at 10:00—typically cookies and juice—and walk down at noon to the house to have lunch with Dad, who would come from the office to eat with us. We'd finish school by 3:00 p.m. I never had a great love for school, and Mom passed down her fear and loathing of all things math to me. I was, however, drawn to a class in Greek mythology. The ancient Greeks' stories of the origin of the world and of the lives and activities of various deities, heroes, and mythological creatures, fascinated me.

Less fascinating was the testing that we endured; we would have to send our completed tests off to Baltimore once a month to be graded. Much to our chagrin, Mom, educated as a teacher, wouldn't let us cheat on the tests. Her love for literature was passed on to us, though, and we were steeped in the adventures of the Bobbsey Twins, the Hardy Boys, Nancy Drew, and other fictional characters.

Mrs. Murray came into our lives when I was eight years old. She stayed with us for four years, even traveling with us to Bartira when we moved there. I'm not sure what happened to her after she left. Despite the many aspects of her character that caused us to either fear her, hate her, or make fun of her (and many times it was a mix of all three), she did have, as I mentioned, some good points. As I look back on those years with Mrs. Murray, I have ambivalent feelings—probably like some military folks have about their boot camp experience. You hate your drill sergeant in the moment, but as time passes, you mellow, the rough edges soften, and you learn to appreciate the drill sergeant's "eccentricities."

Lord knows Mrs. Murray had plenty of *those* to appreciate.

CHAPTER 6

SENHOR OSCAR, CONCEICÃO, AND THE DOMESTICS

IMMIGRATION IS SUCH A HOT-BUTTON TOPIC TODAY, not only in America, but around the world. I grew up technically as an immigrant in the 1960s in Brazil, but my experience there was not what most would think of as today's typical immigrant experience. In Brazil, rather than fleeing from poverty or political or religious corruption or persecution, we willingly embraced our new country and entered into our new lives in Brazil as *chefes,* bosses, rather than as people in difficult circumstances trying to carve out better lives for ourselves. We (well, Mom and Dad) were running the ranches we lived on; we were living in the best houses; we were not, as many immigrants are, dependent on others for work or food or shelter. Being an immigrant in Brazil, being immersed in a culture that was in many ways very different from US culture, was an experience that I wouldn't trade for anything. It allowed me to meet some interesting and wonderful people and learn about customs and practices that I never would have learned in the US.

I first met Conceicão at Mosquito Ranch when I was two years old. Conceicão, whose name means *Conception,* was a heavyset, attractive dark-skinned African woman about fifteen to twenty years older than I was. She was our nursemaid, which is highest on the pecking order of maids. And though she herself was young, she was already a widow;

her husband died from some sort of disease not long after they were married.

In some ways, Conceicão was like an older sister or an aunt to me. She was an excellent seamstress and embroiderer, and she taught me how to both sew and embroider pillowcases, handkerchiefs, and scarves. She did that handiwork for many people in the colony, often in connection with upcoming weddings. I asked her one time why she liked to sew and embroider so much, and she smiled and said, "Because it is my time to create. It is relaxing for me. I would do it all the time if I could."

Indeed, she sewed and embroidered a lot in her spare time, and took me under her wing as I showed interest in what she was doing. She taught me how to use the embroidery hoops, how to thread needles and use the multi-strand floss, how to do running stitches and backstitches and other types of stitches, how to make French knots, and much more. Conceicão was very patient with me, and I took pains to pay attention, because I felt I was learning from the best. (And I certainly knew I was not going to learn how to sew and embroider from my mother, who had neither the time nor the inclination for such activities.)

Conceicão also tried to talk me into starting a hope chest, which all the girls in the colony did. "You need to have a hope chest, Betinha!" she would say.

"Why?"

"To collect the things you need for your future marriage! Do you not want to get married?"

"I don't need a hope chest to get married!" I'd reply. "My mom never had one, and she got married."

Conceicão would tsk-tsk at this; it was evident that I was probably jinxing my marriage by not having a hope chest.

And believe me, Conceicão and many of the other maids who lived in the maids' quarters on our ranches had a healthy fear of jinxes, curses, hexes, and other things that would bring bad luck. Here are just a few of the superstitions they held:

If you eat a mango and wash it down with milk, you will die. (That freaked us kids out at first, but our parents assured us that wasn't true, and proved it by eating mangoes and drinking milk afterward.)

If you sweep someone's feet, that person will never marry.

If you drop a spoon on the floor, a female guest will visit soon. If you drop a fork, a male will visit.

Dropping a knife on the floor is much more serious: it portends a fight will happen. But if you make the sign of the cross, you can prevent the fight.

Never, *never* leave a shoe upside down, unless you want your mother to die. (To tease the maids, I would leave my shoes upside down, causing them to go into a panic and turn them over.)

If you ride bareback, you are not a virgin.

If for some strange reason you wanted the devil to show up, you merely had to buy a new knife and stick it in the base of a banana tree. (Jimmy and I tried this, to no avail.)

Banana trees and knives also factored into something good. If you stick the knife into the trunk at midnight, as you pull the knife out, you will hear the name of your future spouse. (Yes, we tried this. No, it did not work.)

And then there was Saci-pererê (*Black as coal*), a one-legged black or mulatto youngster who smoked a pipe and wore a magical red cape that enabled him to disappear and reappear whenever he wanted. Some believed him to be an annoying prankster; others believed he was malicious and evil. But if you could steal his magic cape, he would grant you a wish. You might even be lucky enough to trap him in a bottle when he was in the form of a dust devil. (Sort of like a more sinister version of *I Dream of Jeannie*.)

Many of these beliefs arose from the Afro-Brazilian religion of Candomblé, which has more than 160,000 followers in Brazil and up to two million worldwide, primarily in South America. The religion recognizes one supreme god and multiple deities (each believer gets his own personal deity that controls his destiny and shapes the person's character). The religion was started in Brazil by slaves who were transported there from West and Central Africa. As time passed, Candomblé, which translates to "dance in honor of the gods," incorporated elements of Roman Catholicism and indigenous Brazilian traditions.

While we kids mercilessly harangued Mrs. Murray, we lovingly teased Conceicão when the opportunity arose. We traveled by train to São Paulo three times a year: when we were on home leave and returning to Texas, for Dad's annual review meeting at the head office, and to go Christmas shopping. On the latter two trips, we kids would have a maid assigned to stay with us. The maids loved these trips as much as we did, because most of them came from small villages and had never been to the big city.

On one such occasion, Theresa and I and Conceicão were assigned a separate sleeper car from Mom and Dad, which was exciting enough in itself. To leave the ranch and take an overnight train to São Paulo, and have our own sleeper? Theresa was just four years old, and I was eight. It didn't get much better than that, in terms of adding a little spice to our lives.

We saw an opportunity to add a bit more spice after Conceicão had a run-in with the steward about the cleanliness of our cabin. The steward, flummoxed and shamefaced, left to get some cleaning items, saying he would be right back.

"I think he likes you," I said to Conceicão, who indignantly shook her head.

"You are being silly," she said. "Stop that nonsense."

Theresa dug an elbow into my side. "I think it's more like *she* likes *him*." We both laughed, further ruffling Conceicão's feathers.

"I most certainly do not!" she said.

The steward returned and cleaned our cabin until Conceicão was satisfied. Theresa and I were laughing and whispering to each other the whole time, while Conceicão was giving us a stern eye.

"So sorry, *Senhora*," the steward said after he was finished. "It is good now?"

Conceicão nodded and the man left. In a bit, Conceicão ordered bottled water for us, and the steward returned with the water. This time he was all smiles, figuring he was now in Conceicão's good graces. To Theresa and me, he said, "Is this your first time going to São Paulo?"

"Oh no, we've been many times before," I said, trying to sound like a world traveler.

The man raised his eyebrows in mock surprise and turned to Conceicão. "And you, *Senhora*? Have you been many times, too?"

Conceicão hesitated, then said "Not so many."

"Ah! Well, I hope you can take in the Municipal Theater. It was modeled after the Paris Opéra and is quite magnificent. And Ibirapuera Park should be gorgeous this time of year. It is actually beautiful year-round."

"Oh yes, we go to those places and many more all the time," Theresa said, taking my cue and trying to act about twenty years older than she was.

The man chuckled. "These two, I bet they keep you hopping," he said.

"Oh, they do that," Conceicão said acidly. "Thank you for the water," she said, ending the conversation. The man bowed and exited our cabin, but he likely heard Theresa's and my peals of laughter as he walked down the aisle.

"Maybe we should invite him to come with us, so you can have a companion in São Paulo," I said.

"We should find out if he's married," Theresa added. "He looked pretty interested in you."

Conceicão tried to ignore us, but we wouldn't let the "budding romance" die. We pressed the call button several times after the lights had gone out, and the steward showed up each time, asking what we needed. Conceicão didn't know we were pressing the button—and of course we never fessed up—so Conceicão assumed he was just bothering us because indeed he did have a crush on her. She finally told him to stop bothering us or she would report him. He apologized profusely while Theresa and I tried to muffle our giggles in our pillows.

On another train journey to São Paulo, we were accompanied by a very pretty maid named Cida. She was one of the youngest maids we had and had never been anywhere but a few small towns near Mosquito and the ranch itself. Cida was a bit shy and unsure of herself, but Mom and Dad thought it would be a great experience for her to see the big city. Our whole family, along with Cida, were together during the day in São Paulo, but in the evening, Theresa and I and Cida had our own room in our downtown hotel. We played the same game we had with Conceicão, ordering room service and then calling the bellhop back a few times for items we needed, such as ketchup or more bottled water. He made four or five trips in all, and we would throw in little comments like "Isn't she pretty?" He would smile and reply, "Ela é muito bonita" ("She is very beautiful"), which would make Cida blush and look away.

Cida, being younger and shyer than Conceicão—she was just a few years older than me, and was Michael's nursemaid—had less control over us. One evening we got into it with her in our hotel room.

"We don't want to be stuck in this room!" I said. "We are in São Paulo—we should get to see the city!"

"Não, não, fica aqui!" ("No, no, you stay here!") Cida was frightened of the big city, of getting lost or mugged. (And of course, our parents didn't want us wandering the streets of São Paulo, either.) She didn't even like looking out our sixth-story window, because she had never been up so high.

"Fine, then we're going to jump out this window!" Theresa said as she opened the window and stuck one leg partially over the sill.

"Não, volte para dentro!" ("No, get back inside!") Cida shrieked. I can still see the look of panic on her face. We kept threatening to jump, and eventually she broke down and cried before we stopped tormenting her.

While we liked Cida (despite how we sometimes treated her!), Conceicão was our—and Mom's—favorite maid. Conceicão was like Mom's first lieutenant, her trusted leader of the maid ranks. When Conceicão would suggest that Mom hire certain women, more often than not Mom would hire them, and they would turn out to be good hires. Conceicão, who spoke fluent Portuguese, was the perfect intermediary between the ranch help and Mom; she was essentially Mom's ears and voice in communicating with the help.

One aspect of Conceicão's personality that drew her to Mom was her delight in collecting and sharing gossip about the other maids and the people living in the colony. Mom never met a tidbit of gossip that she didn't like, and she and Conceicão would sit for hours in the kitchen, drinking iced tea or coffee and talking about the latest in the lives of those living around them. In this way, Conceicão served as Mom's eyes and ears on the ranch. Through Conceicão, Mom learned that a family of albinos thought God was making them white; she was privy to birth control issues among the maids and to who was sleeping with whom; and she discovered who worked hard even when not being watched and who got by with as little work as possible.

Their other favorite pastime was listening to *O Direito de Nascer* (*The Right to be Born*), a popular, daily, hour-long soap opera on the radio. Mom would always make sure that school was finished by then so she, Conceicão, and the other maids could listen to the program. The cook would sit in on these sessions, too. Dad, of course—with his father's blood flowing through his veins—would laugh at Mom, saying didn't she have better things to do. To which she would reply, "It helps with my Portuguese." Dad would continue to tease her, but Mom, of course, would never back down.

CHAPTER 6

One summer afternoon, Conceicão came up to my mother, who was writing a letter in the kitchen.

"Dona Mary Lee!" she said, "I have some bad news for you."

Mom put her pen down and braced herself; she could tell by Conceicão's tone that something serious had happened.

"It's Elsa," Conceicão said. "She's pregnant."

This was indeed bad news. Elsa was a young and very beautiful housemaid with long black hair and green eyes; she turned heads everywhere she went. Elsa's parents, knowing this and knowing that their daughter could be easily persuaded, sat down and had a long talk with my mother before they allowed Elsa to be hired at the ranch.

"You must keep an eye on her," Elsa's father said. "She is young and naïve, and I know what the men on a ranch are like."

"Please, Dona Mary Lee," Elsa's mom pleaded, "Don't let anything bad happen to my baby. Can we entrust her to you? She has always lived with us. If she comes here, we fear she might not make the best decisions."

"You have no need to worry," my mother said. "I'll make sure she's safe. This will be a good experience for her."

Mom could tell that neither parent was fully convinced, but they gave their approval for Elsa to be hired.

Now, less than a year after that conversation, Elsa was pregnant.

"Who did it?" Mom demanded. "Who got her pregnant?"

"Agostino."

"Agostino! I'm not surprised. I never did like his character." Agostino was the gardener. According to Mom, he was a knowledgeable gardener but worked slowly and had a poor attitude. "Where is he now? I need a word with him."

"That's just it, Dona Mary Lee. He has picked up his paycheck and is now headed into town. He said he is not planning on coming back."

My mother's eyes flashed as she sprang into action. No two-bit gardener was going to pull the wool over her eyes—not to mention Elsa's.

She quickly placed a phone call to the ranch office. In her best Portuguese, she yelled "Não deixe o caminhão sair! Não deixe o caminhão sair!" This means "Do not let the truck leave!" Only, in my mother's broken Portuguese, it came out more like "No day shoe camoan sy ear!," which was somewhat close to the right pronunciation . . . somewhat. I had wandered into the room and saw that Conceicão, even though she was worried, was trying to suppress a grin at my mother's comical pronunciation, made all the more humorous by her wild gesticulations as she spoke and the bulging vein in her neck.

Eventually the office understood what she was saying and they successfully stopped the truck. Meanwhile, Mom sped to the office in her own car, slamming on her brakes behind the truck, bouncing out from behind the wheel, and striding up to the truck. Agostino, seeing her approach, sank a bit as he sat behind the truck's wheel.

"Get out!" she commanded him.

"Leave?" he said, hopeful.

"No. Get out of the truck. Now!"

Agostino dutifully got out of the truck, looking fretful.

"Dona Mary Lee, I was just going into—"

"I know what you were doing! And I know what you did! You got Elsa pregnant. She's a mere child! You took advantage of her!"

"Oh no, Dona Mary Lee. I did not force anything on her. We professed our love for each other."

My mother sneered. "Your love! Try 'your lust.' And if you love her then why did you tell people you were leaving the ranch for good? Without giving me notice, I might add?"

Agostino had no good answer for this one. He seemed to be searching the distant hills for a response, but none came.

"Do you plan to marry Elsa?"

That snapped his eyes back toward her in astonishment. "Marry! I never said nothing about marrying her. She is, like you say, a child. Too young to marry."

"But not too young to knock up."

"Knock up? What is this 'knock up'?"

"Get pregnant."

"It is not good, I admit, but sometimes this happens when two people are in . . . when two people get together." He did not dare say *in love* again.

"So you knock up a child, you grab your paycheck, and you try to leave the ranch. For good. Without telling me, your boss."

He looked like a sorrowful dog being chewed out by its owner.

"Do you plan on helping this girl out?" my mother asked.

"Helping her out? You mean with money? I am a man of meager means, Dona Mary Lee. Surely you know that."

Of meager and *devious* means, my mother no doubt thought.

"Give me your paycheck." She stuck out her hand, wiggling her fingers impatiently.

"What?" the astonished man said.

"Your paycheck. Hand it over. It's going to Elsa. It's the very least she deserves. And believe me, she deserves a lot better than a lazy gardener like you."

"But Dona Mary Lee . . . "

"Give it to me or I'll call the authorities and tell them what you did to this young child."

His eyes darkened as he thought over his possibilities. Money was near and dear to him, but so was his life, and he probably thought it was a fifty-fifty chance of escaping with his if he disobeyed my mother.

Grumbling, he handed over his paycheck.

"Now, get the hell out of here. You're fired."

My mother's reputation with the maids was already high, because though she could be stern with them, she treated them well and fairly. This incident launched her into the hero stratosphere. She became an instant legend for how she stopped, stood up to, and stuck it to Agostino.

At both Bartira and Mosquito we had houseboys. They were in charge of serving meals and of the floral arrangements in the living room and dining room, of tending and restocking the liquor inventory, and of shining the silver and my dad's boots, among other duties. Mom taught Aniba, our houseboy at Mosquito, to drive, so he could drive the maids to the colony or drive to the office to pick something up. But he would only drive on the ranch, as he of course was not licensed. (We also had a ranch driver who would do the driving for the ranch—to doctor's appointments, on ranch errands, and to basically wherever we needed to go, such as my piano lessons in Presidente Prudente and orthodontist appointments in Londrina, though I would have been happy to give those up.)

Candido, our houseboy at Bartira, was my favorite. Candido was short and always had a big smile on his face. He loved to tease and joke, and didn't mind being kidded about his height, so I called him *baixinho* (shorty), and he would tease me right back.

We had a wonderful relationship; I used to love to just sit and talk with him while he set the table or did some other sort of work around the house. The only time he was serious was when he was serving dinner; I couldn't get him to crack a smile then, no matter how hard I tried. (And I did try, even to the point of nearly tipping over his serving platter on several occasions. He would deftly move the platter out of my reach, move away while ignoring me, and keep on serving.)

Candido was one of those people who lifted your spirits whenever you were around them. The only person he *didn't* get along with was Conceicão, who was jealous of Candido, because the houseboy was at the top of the pecking order among the household help. Conceicão was Mom's favorite, but she still ranked below Candido, and that rankled her no end. So they were always at each other, making snide comments and put-downs. Behind her back, Candido would sometimes call Conceicão a *bale* (whale), because Conceicão was, as I mentioned, on the larger side. Candido, for his part, was fit and trim and always looked about ten years younger than he really was. He was also a rather natty dresser;

on Sundays he would put on his best clothes and top it off with a large Stetson hat, and he and his wife and kids—all taller than he was—would attend the soccer matches that took place on Sundays. You could spot him from a mile away in that gigantic Stetson of his. (It had become a long-standing tradition that the general manager of the ranches would bring Candido a new Stetson after going back home for leave. Later, when Dad became GM and gifted Candido with a new Stetson, he was at least the third such GM to do so, adding to the diminutive man's cache of first-class cowboy hats. Candido was barely five feet tall, but he walked much taller in his huge Stetsons. To me, it looked rather comical, but I never kidded him about it, because he was such a sweet man.)

Candido was illiterate but had a sharp mind and great memory and found ways to get his job done. For example, in keeping the liquor stocked, he would painstakingly copy the bottle labels so he would know what to order. (Too bad he didn't have a smartphone to take a snapshot with!) Mom tried to get both Conceicão and him to take night classes to learn to read and write, and they did enroll, but they both stopped going once they learned how to sign their names.

On each ranch we had one or more people designated to drive us into Rancharia or Presidente Prudente for shopping, errands, and appointments. (And to São Paulo and Campinas, where I went to boarding school at age fourteen.) At Bartira we had two drivers, Amadeus and his younger brother Sabia. Sabia was fearful of my mom, and never seemed to be able to please her—if she sent him into town to pick up some things, invariably he returned with the wrong items or inferior brands—but Amadeus was held in high esteem by my mother. He was calm and easygoing, and he was Mom's other great source of colony and maid gossip. Between Amadeus and Conceicão, my mother was very well informed about the goings-on of those living in the colonies and serving in the house. It was our version of *Entertainment Tonight* or the *National Enquirer.*

It was a combination of Amadeus's smooth and affable demeanor, his ability to deliver juicy gossip, and his knack for bringing home the items my mother actually wanted that endeared him to her. As a result, he had the rather startling capacity for swaying my mother's opinions and decisions on matters. This set him apart from all others on the ranch—sometimes including my father.

While Amadeus was, as I say, normally unruffled and relaxed, there were two times when I saw him with a panic-stricken look on his face.

The first time was when he drove Mom and me to our dentist appointments in Rancharia. He dropped us off and headed off to a supermarket to do some shopping. The plan was for us to walk outside the dentist's office when we were finished, where he would be parked and waiting.

Well, when we walked outside after our appointments, there was no sign of Amadeus. We looked up and down the block but could not find our car.

"Come on," my mom grumbled. "Let's see if we can find him."

We walked around the downtown streets to no avail. After a while we headed back toward the dentist's office—and saw our car parked on the corner with no one in it.

Muttering a few choice words that singed my delicate ears, Mom headed toward the car with me in tow. To her further consternation, the keys were in the ignition.

"I do not believe this!" Mom growled. "What is he doing, leaving the keys in the ignition? He's just inviting someone to steal our car!"

As if to prove her point, she snarled "Get in."

I got in the passenger seat, and she got behind the wheel and drove off. We circled the block, looking for our AWOL driver, and found him back where we started: in front of the dentist's office, where the car had been parked.

His eyes grew big and his jaw dropped when he saw Mom swing into a parking spot and stop abruptly, causing the tires to squeal.

Mom instructed me to get in the back seat, got out of the car, and walked around to the passenger side, glaring at Amadeus.

"Where were you?" she barked. "We've been looking for you for half an hour."

It was probably about ten minutes, but I didn't think Mom was in a very correctable mood at the moment, so I let that pass.

"I'm so sorry!" Amadeus spluttered. "There was a long line at the supermarket, it was very crowded. I came back as soon as I could and parked and ran up to the dentist's office to see if I could find you!"

"Leaving the keys in the ignition? For anyone on the street to steal?"

"No, well, I, I . . . yes, I guess I did, but I wasn't thinking because I was in such a rush to find you!"

Mom rolled her eyes and sighed. "Next time, be here on time. At the very least, keep the keys with you!"

"Yes, *Senhora*," he said, a hangdog expression on his face.

All the way home, Amadeus was tense and quiet, very unusual for him.

The other time Amadeus probably wanted to crawl under a rock also involved a car—a brand-new Chevy Veraneio, a big, boxy Suburban. But this time just he, Michael, and I were involved. That Mom was not there turned out to be a *huge* blessing for Amadeus.

He had driven us into Rancharia, where Michael had a judo lesson. I went along to get off the ranch and have a little fun. Turns out I had more fun in the beginning than the end.

I was fifteen years old and knew how to drive but did not have a license yet (you had to be eighteen to get a driver's license in Brazil). After Amadeus dropped Michael off, I begged and pleaded with Amadeus to let me drive in town while he went to the corner bar where some of his ranch friends were playing cards. We had seen a few ranch cars in front of the bar on our way to the center of town.

"You're the life of the party, Amadeus, you know that," I said as we drove slowly down a downtown street. "They would love to have you."

"No."

"But this is a time for you to relax with your friends, not hang out with a fifteen-year-old girl."

"No."

"You know that I'm an excellent driver, that I've driven lots of times on the ranch."

"No."

"I've never had even a minor accident behind the wheel. I'm an extremely careful driver."

"No."

"But I've been driving since I was fourteen!"

"No."

I sullenly sank back in my seat and sighed in frustration. I had thought this was going to be easier. I could usually sweet-talk men into allowing me to do things that women like Mom and Conceicão would never let me do.

"Well, let's go to that bar, anyway," I grumbled. "I can have a Coke and *coxhina* and stare out the window for two hours while we wait for Michael and his stupid judo lesson. You can hang out with your friends." (*Coxhina* was Brazilian chicken croquettes.)

In a few minutes, we found ourselves in this bar, which was dark and loud and filled with blue collar workers. *Sertanejo* (backcountry) music played in the background. A few of the ranchers recognized me and asked me what I was doing. I sulkily told them my sad story of not being allowed to drive. A couple of them gave Amadeus a hard time, and he finally relented. But before he handed me the keys he said, "You know if you damage this car, we are both in very big trouble."

I did, of course, know that. And I knew the trouble would be increased because the car was brand-new, one my Mom had just bought for the ranch.

"I told you I've never been in an accident before! Just trust me," I said.

Famous last words.

"One hour," he said. "You be back here in one hour, and we will go get Michael."

I nodded, smiled, and skipped off. I had never felt so old or mature as I sat behind the wheel of this brand-new Suburban, took in that new car smell, and started the engine. I tuned the radio to a Brazilian rock station and pulled away from the curb.

My elation turned to trepidation as I began to slowly maneuver through the narrow streets of Rancharia—made all the narrower by cars parked on both sides. Most of the streets were one way, but even these had barely enough for our large car to squeeze through. I gripped the wheel tightly with my now sweaty hands.

But I made it to the local bakery after several nervous minutes, and hung out with some of my friends there, having a croissant and some coffee and relaxing a bit. Before I returned to the bar, however, one of my friends, knowing I didn't have a license, cautioned me to drive on some side streets going back in case cops were out. I thought this was a good idea.

It was dark by this time, and in trying to navigate a less-traveled way back to the bar, I found myself on streets I had never been on. A bit flustered, and not quite certain where I was going, I turned the wrong way down a one-way street. That was a minor, correctable mistake.

The bigger mistake happened just seconds after I turned, though. I heard a grating crunch of metal on metal and slammed on the brakes. I had hit a car, an old junker, that was up on blocks and parked in the street. In fact, I had partially knocked the car off its blocks. It sat there, tilted on one side, a sad-looking shell of a vehicle. My heart was thumping so loud I could hear it; I was panic-stricken and breathing rapidly.

I surveyed the damage done to our car; it was scratched and dented a bit on the front driver's side, but in my mind, it was crumpled like a tin can. Amadeus's words came back to me: *You know if you damage this car, we are both in very big trouble.*

"Oh shit, oh shit, oh shit, oh shit," I said, but that didn't seem to help matters any. My hands were shaking. Neighborhood dogs, hearing the sound of the crash, had started barking. A few people began wandering over to see what had happened. They murmured among themselves and looked at me and the cars but didn't say anything directly to me.

Running away didn't seem like a bad option. I could catch a bus to São Paulo, get a job as a waitress, live in a little flat above the café where I worked. Maybe change my name in case my parents came looking for me to punish me.

But after several deep breaths, a little voice in my head told me that running away was probably not the best option. Besides, I didn't really want to be a waitress.

So, after one more deep breath, I walked rather unsteadily to the house nearest the heap of junk that I had hit. I knocked on the door, visions of an angry potbellied man in a sweat-stained undershirt opening the door, telling his pack of barking, slavering Rottweilers to shut up.

No one answered.

Slightly relieved, I went next door and knocked. An old man with wild white hair sticking every which way opened the door and stared quizzically at me. He probably didn't get a whole lot of white fifteen-year-old girls knocking on his door most evenings.

I told him what happened and he said, "That is Francisco's car. It's just an old junker. I wouldn't worry about it."

I felt a bit of relief. And even more when he said, "It's *your* car I would worry about. He hasn't driven that thing in five years. He probably won't even notice it's off its blocks."

Emboldened by this, I insisted on leaving my name, phone, and address for Francisco. The man shrugged and said he would deliver the message to Francisco.

That hurdle over, I went to my next big hurdle: facing Amadeus. I drove to the bar, walked in, and Amadeus could see by the look on my face that his worst fear was realized.

"You got in an accident!" he said. It was an accusation, not a question. He could see I was not injured, so any concern that way quickly turned into wrath—some for himself for letting me drive, but most for me for banging up the new car, which he ran out to inspect.

He muttered "Mãe de Deus" (mother of God) under his breath when he saw the damage. "No, no, no, no, no." He put his hand up to his eyes, perhaps hoping the damage would miraculously disappear, but it didn't.

I explained it all to him and he drove us back to the scene of the accident. "Why oh why did you give this man your name and address?" he said, as if I had just passed national security secrets to the Russians. "What were you thinking?"

I was thinking I should own up and do the right thing, but I didn't say this, because I knew he wouldn't care a whit about my conscientious and, I thought, commendable behavior.

We drove to get Michael, who had been waiting for a while by this time, and his sullenness at being made to wait turned into evil joy when he found out the reason for the delay. He chortled that I was going to get in trouble big time, that I'd probably be grounded for a year. I thanked him for his concern and we drove home, Amadeus and I in a bad mood, Michael enjoying the fact that his big sister was soon going to catch hell.

Mom and Dad, gratefully, were in São Paulo on business and wouldn't be home for a few days. But that didn't stop my mind from racing: What would I do if Francisco told the authorities? How would I pay for the damage to his car and ours? Would Mom and Dad disown me? What was my punishment going to be? Could I go live with my grandparents in Texas?

The next morning, sure enough, Francisco was at our ranch office, demanding money to repair his junker. Our bookkeeper suggested we pay him in meat, which Francisco was happy with; our butcher promised to keep the transaction quiet. I would pay the ranch for the meat from my own money, and no one would be the wiser. His junker had just earned him a lot of freshly butchered meat, probably more meat than he would buy in several months' time.

Our ranch mechanics were able to get the dents out of our car, but the paint was a custom order that could only be purchased in São Paulo.

Thank you, Mom, for buying a car with custom paint! If not for that, Mom and Dad never would have known a thing about the accident.

I barely slept that night, rehearsing my apologies and excuses to my parents. My stomach was in knots as I sat that next morning in the kitchen with the maids for my parents to arrive back at the ranch. They were treating me kindly, trying to console me. I felt like a death row inmate waiting to be walked to her execution. As soon as Mom and Dad walked in the kitchen, I stood up and burst into tears. I told them what happened, and to my relief they were not angry with me. Michael had slunk in to the kitchen with an evil grin on his face to watch the fireworks; the grin faded when he saw Mom and Dad actually console me.

"You shouldn't be driving in town without a license; you know that," Dad said. My mother shot Amadeus, who was standing nearby, a withering glance, and he hung his head in shame.

"I know," I said. I looked quickly at Amadeus. "Don't blame Amadeus. It wasn't his fault. I begged him mercilessly until he finally gave in."

Only Amadeus could have gotten away with this, because he was so strongly in my mother's favor.

"Never again," she said sharply to both of us.

"Never again!" we both replied.

My dad really wasn't mad about the accident. After all, accidents happen. But he was absolutely *livid* when word somehow leaked back to him that I had paid Francisco in meat. He had rarely been that mad with me.

"But I plan to pay for the meat with my own money," I said, my voice small and my legs quaking. "I wasn't just giving it away."

"That's not the point!" he said. "The point is, that meat is *company property*. You do not pay off your own debts with *company property*. Why didn't you just come to me about it?"

Meekly, I said, "Because you and Mom weren't home yet. And the guy was here, demanding payment. I didn't know what to do. I didn't have enough money to pay him off immediately, so I thought . . . "

"Well, you thought *wrong*," he snapped. "I am very disappointed in you."

I slunk away, feeling about two inches tall. I know, looking back, that he was right, but his tongue-lashing stuck with me for a long, long time. In fact, it still makes me feel bad when I think about it.

I would be remiss if I didn't mention Conceicão's father, Senhor Oscar, as we kids knew him. The ranch had hired Senhor Oscar to manage the port area by the Paranapanema River, which was the southernmost boundary of Mosquito Ranch.

The port was important to the ranch because we ferried the cattle across the river into the state of Parana. The ferry was also used for local traffic and for the bus that went from Presidente Prudente to Londrina in Parana. Before the ferry system was put in place, the cattle had to swim across the river, which was about a half mile wide and was dangerous for two reasons: the current was swift, and could easily carry them off or drown them, and if they didn't drown, the piranha might feast on them. To alleviate the latter problem, the ranch hands would choose a sick or old cow, kill it by stabbing it, and shove it in the river to attract the piranha, which would devour it while the other cows crossed safely upstream. But this all happened before we arrived; the ferry system was in place when we lived on Mosquito Ranch.

Senhor Oscar was dark-skinned, tall, and lanky. He lived in a white wooden house up on stilts near the river, and part of his duties as port manager was to collect rent from the sharecroppers who lived nearby. He would walk through the jungle by the river, looking for squatters or any other issues; the ranch supplied him with a radio for calls if he needed to report problems.

When we knew him, Senhor Oscar wasn't married, but he always seemed to have plenty of women around him. He had a certain charisma to him, a certain charm and authority, that got women's attention and that gained the respect of the men he came in contact with.

We loved going down to the river because life was so different just twelve miles away from our ranch house. The river area was populated by fifty or so people who lived in huts and sharecropped the land. Swift-King had set up this sharecropping system in part to take care of the squatter problem.

On the way to the port, my dad would often stop at the rather run-down *boteco* (bar) just before the river. It was a roadhouse inn with some rooms above the bar. He would stop to get us kids some candy and to buy some tobacco for the sharecroppers who lived along the river. They rolled their own tobacco and always appreciated it when my dad brought them some.

When we arrived at the port, my dad would give the sharecroppers the tobacco, and then he would go to Senhor Oscar's house and sit down on one of the two benches at the rustic wooden table in the main room with him to talk over matters. We kids would usually explore along the river and play with the sharecroppers' kids, but occasionally we would go inside the house. The hardwood floors were unfinished and unpainted, and you could see light seeping between the boards, which were far from airtight. The windows had no screens, and were left open during the day; insects and the occasional bird were his constant companions. Nearly everything in the house was made of wood, which was bleached because of the constant cleaning with homemade lye soap.

Senhor Oscar would give us fish to take back to the ranch—bottom feeders with their mouths on the bottom of their bodies, which freaked us out a bit. He would also offer my dad various home remedies.

"How are your joints? Are they aching?" he would ask.

"Oh, no, they're good," my dad would quickly respond. He didn't want anything to do with Senhor Oscar's mysterious ointments and liquids.

"Do you have headaches? Or trouble breathing?" Senhor Oscar would say.

"No, no, I'm healthy as a horse," my father would reply.

"Your horse? It is sick?" Senhor Oscar would say, a look of concern on his face. My father's Portuguese was good, but it wasn't perfect.

"No. Horses are healthy, I am healthy," Dad would say.

"I have *pinga,*" Senhor Oscar would say, holding up a bottle. "The best cure there is for rheumatoid arthritis. You drink?"

"No, no, I'm good," my dad would say, waving his hands in front of his face. No way did he want to drink from that bottle, which was full of dead fire ants and distilled alcohol made from fermented sugarcane juice. It was Senhor Oscar's homemade concoction, and the word was it was extremely strong. My dad joked that it was probably strong enough to raise the dead, though the drink might kill them again in the process. Some of the nicknames for *pinga,* we later learned, were *abre-coração* (heart opener), *água-benta* (holy water), *bafo-de-tigre* (tiger breath), and *limpa-olho* (eye wash).

"I have *pinga* in the morning and at night," Senhor Oscar told my dad. "It keeps me healthy."

Indeed, Senhor Oscar died an old, old man—possibly over one hundred years old—but no one, including him, knew his age.

Many times when we went to the river, we would fish with cane poles for piranha. We'd put them in big quart peach cans. Jimmy once stuck his finger in a can with a freshly-caught piranha in it and the fish ripped off the tip of his finger. Dad wrapped it in a handkerchief and Senhor Oscar hustled to his house, returning with some mystery ointment that he dabbed on the wound, with a tearful and dubious Jimmy looking on. But the ointment must have worked; at least Jimmy didn't get an infection—though he did have to learn how to live without the tip of his finger.

The "river people," as I called them, could count well enough to handle their money, but none of them—including Senhor Oscar—could read or write. The ranch eventually built a school and hired teachers for the river people so that the next generation would become literate.

We were fascinated by their way of life. They came from the sugarcane fields in the state of Parana, which was immediately south of the river. Their ancestors came from Africa, brought over as slaves to work the fields (Brazil was the last country in the Western world to abolish slavery, back in 1888; about 40 percent of the slaves that were brought to the Americas—about four million total—were imported to Brazil).

The women looked distinctly different from other Brazilian women; they had their hair tied up and wore white scarves or turbans on their heads. They made corn meal using a *pilao* (pestle) to grind the corn in a hollow drum. They also hulled rice and ground manioc, a tuberous root, into flour. We would stand back a bit and watch them work in the hot sun; they would be talking and laughing, and sometimes they would sing songs in either Portuguese or some African language that I of course didn't know. They seemed to always be outside, always be working, and somehow always maintaining the energy they needed to accomplish their work under a very hot sun.

Theirs was a work ethic and a lifestyle that would have pleased Buck Emmert.

CHAPTER 7

MOVING UP THE LADDER

I LEARNED, OF COURSE, a lot of life lessons while growing up in Brazil. Many of those lessons were unique to the people and the Brazilian culture. But a few I would have learned regardless of where we lived.

One was that my mother, bless her soul, was always scheming. (May I remind you of her setting up Dad's interview in Chicago with Swift, without his knowledge, which landed us in Brazil in the first place?)

Another was that sometimes being the kid sucked.

Those two lessons were entwined in one decision (a very unpopular one with me) to move from Mosquito Ranch to Bartira Ranch. This happened in 1969, when I was eleven years old.

Mom always had designs on Dad becoming general manager of all five Swift-King ranches in Brazil. (Dad was ambivalent about the prospects, fearing he'd be weighed down in paperwork as a GM, but that didn't seem to concern my mother any.) When Monte Irwin, the GM when we moved to Brazil, retired in 1967, Mom pounced.

"This is it!" she told my dad. "This is our big chance!"

"Our big chance for what?" Dad said.

"For you to become general manager!"

"I don't know. I wouldn't mind it—except I'd probably be stuck behind a desk most of the time. And when I wasn't behind a desk, I'd be in meetings in São Paulo. I think that would drive me crazy."

No matter how Mom tried to cajole and convince him, Dad was, at best, halfhearted about the idea. To my mother's great disappointment and chagrin, their good friend, Ed Lasater, was named GM of the ranches. She wasn't at all upset with Ed, and my parents remained close friends with the Lasaters. She simply wanted the bigger title, the better pay, the move upward—a move that would have meant having a phone where she could place calls to the US and anywhere she pleased; having electricity 24/7, with no need to turn off a generator each night to save electricity; Rancharia, a decent-sized town, was only twenty minutes away; and it was only one hour to Presidente Prudente, with over half the road paved asphalt. These all seemed like relative luxuries to her.

As fate would have it, Ed Lasater stayed in the GM position for two years. Then, he and his wife, Anne, moved back to Texas in 1969, partly for their kids' education and partly because Anne was less than enthralled with living in Brazil. So the higher-ups approached Dad about his interest in becoming GM.

"I'll talk it over with Mary Lee," he told them. Not that he needed a conversation with her to know her thinking on the matter.

I'll never forget the fateful day I overheard a bit of a rather heated conversation between my parents about the matter. I was in the dining room, which had a double-sided fireplace shared with the living room; we often snuck into the dining room to hear conversations between our parents. I couldn't see my mom, but I could hear the agitation in her voice.

"You can't pass up this opportunity *twice,*" she said. "Don't you want to move up? Don't you want to be the main boss?"

That was an easy one for my dad to answer. "No! I told you before I don't want to push pencils and take NoDoz to stay awake in some godforsaken office!"

"They're not just going to stick you in some office! You'll still be in charge of five ranches."

"They brought me down here to do what I'm doing: raising cattle and reforming these pastures. I've done a hell of a job doing that."

"Exactly! Which is why you should become GM! So you can spread that knowledge around and make sure it happens on all five ranches."

"Look, last time we went through this, I got a raise. I plan to ask for another one at this meeting. We're doing fine here."

"*You're* doing fine here! I'm not! You deserve to be the GM! We should be at Bartira with you overseeing all the ranches! Why manage one when you can manage all five? You know they love you! If you pushed for that position, they'd give it to you in a heartbeat! This is our chance to move up!"

My father sighed in frustration. It was never easy arguing with my mother. She would have made a great courtroom lawyer.

I slunk away, mumbling a few desperate prayers as I did and trying to convince myself that Dad would win this battle, as he had won the last one when the GM position became open. I knew you couldn't talk my mother into anything if she didn't want it herself, but my Dad was no pushover, either. He wasn't as outwardly demonstrative in his willfulness and stubbornness as my mother—few were—but he was a deeply resolute man who knew who he was and what he wanted. He couldn't be coaxed or wheedled into something he didn't want.

I kept telling myself that.

So, imagine my surprise when he came home one summer afternoon not long after that overheard conversation and announced to us kids: "Get ready for a move. I've been named general manager of all five ranches. We're going to Bartira."

I was livid. I didn't want to move. I loved my life and my friends on Mosquito Ranch, and I blamed my mother for pushing Dad into the GM position. But I took a closer look at my dad and saw the genuine joy and excitement on his face, and I realized that as much as Mom had pressed him to go for the job, in the end it was his decision.

That made the news slightly more palatable. Slightly.

The main reason I didn't want to move was I had made some good friends at Mosquito. We had settled in and I was at an age where friendships started to deepen, where peers rose in importance, and independence was starting to sprout wings. Now, those friendships were going to be severed, or at least severely hampered, by this abominable move to Bartira.

Zenia was the best friend I had growing up in Brazil. She was very pretty, very feminine, with long black hair and light skin. Zenia was my age, the daughter of the ranch foreman, who bore a lot of responsibility at Mosquito: Henrique was in charge of the machine shop, the sawmill, the water pumps, and a lot more. But his biggest contribution to the ranch, in my estimation, was having Zenia as his daughter.

Zenia and I had so much fun together. We each had these three-foot-tall dolls, and we would do sleepovers where we would build a makeshift house under a mango tree, using sticks and branches to fashion the walls. We'd even create our own little "wood-burning stove" in our "kitchen," using a few bricks and bits of wood, which we would ignite with oil and matches. We would heat up rice and beans in old peach cans over the fire and have our dinner in our house under the tree.

One day, Zenia and I decided we needed to baptize our gigantic dolls. Her mother had made white veils for the occasion. As we were under our mango tree, discussing how to conduct the baptism, Jimmy wandered by and Zenia's eyes lit up. I could tell she had a great idea.

"Jimmy! Come here!"

He came over, curious. He liked playing with us, when we let him, which wasn't often. But he didn't like doing what he would call "girly stuff."

"What?" he said.

"We're going to baptize our dolls! We want you to be the *padrinho*!"

Jimmy scoffed; no way was he going to be the "godfather" of two very large dolls.

"*Você é louco!*" he said, walking away.

Zenia shouted that *he* was the crazy one and that he would never make a good godfather anyway. We both laughed, and we baptized our godfather-less dolls, pouring water over their heads.

Zenia and I were inseparable from the age of four to eleven, when my family left Mosquito. I had sleepovers at her house, though I preferred that she sleep at our house, because her mom would shut all the windows at night so we wouldn't breathe in the "night air" and get bronchitis. It could get awfully stuffy in the summer with no air circulating! Her mom also wouldn't allow Zenia to wash her hair at night, because then she would go to bed with damp hair and invite sickness in. Zenia would roll her eyes at things like this, but she was close to her mother.

We did everything together. We even graduated from dolls to real babies—not ours, of course, but those of women in the colony, who allowed us to carry them around a bit. We loved that until they either started crying or soiled their diapers; then we quickly returned them to their mothers.

About a year after we moved to Bartira, Zenia's parents drove up to that ranch for a three-day visit with Zenia's grandparents; her grandfather was foreman at Bartira. I was thrilled to be able to see my good friend. Zenia's dad and grandfather would talk about their work on the ranches, comparing notes and giving updates, and her mom and grandmother would share the gossip from each ranch.

My dad always thought very highly of Zenia's father, Henrique, who was both hardworking and intelligent. The year we moved to Bartira, he quit working for the Swift-King operation in Brazil because he didn't get along with the new manager at Mosquito. He had saved enough money that he was able to start his own milk route; he quickly grew the business from one to four or five routes. He was doing well with the routes, but his life changed rather dramatically, as I learned from Zenia about a year after our move to Bartira.

I can still remember the moment. Mom and I were headed to a seamstress in Rancharia; it was a sunny Saturday morning. She was taking just me with her, and I treasured the alone time with her, which I didn't get all that often. As Amadeus was pulling the car up to the house to pick us up, the phone rang in our living room. At first, I was irritated to be slowed by the phone; I figured it was one of Mom's friends, and they would gab for twenty minutes or so. My eyes lit up when Mom told me it was Zenia as she handed me the phone.

We chatted as we normally did for a few minutes, but she sounded sort of breathless, like she had exciting news. She finally could hold it in no longer.

"Guess what?" she said.

"What?"

"You know how my dad plays the *loteria esportiva*? The one that's on TV every Sunday night?"

"Yeah."

"Well, he won! He won a lot of money!"

"Oh, that's so cool! I can't believe it!"

In the *loteria esportiva* (sports lottery), you picked the outcomes of the thirteen national soccer games that were played each week. A silly, animated zebra (there are no zebras in Brazil—except, I guess, for this one) would declare which lottery columns were successful as an announcer gave the results. There was even a saying in Brazil: *deu zebra*, which essentially means "that didn't work out." It was beyond silly—but half the nation was glued to their TVs on Sunday nights to see if they won.

We giggled and laughed, and I was very happy for her. It felt almost like *we* had won the lottery. With the winnings, her dad did what he always said he would do: he bought them a big house (they had their own maids!) and a new car. They skipped several rungs on the socioeconomic ladder and were able to live in comfort and style. Typical of Zenia's dad, though, he kept working his milk routes—though he added routes and drivers to expand his business. Working hard was a core part of who he was, and no amount of money was going to change that.

I cried the entire two-hour drive from Mosquito to Bartira (which we undertook in Dad's brand-new company car, a Veranaro, a suburban with air-conditioning). With each passing mile I missed Zenia and my life at Mosquito more. I had grown close to the maids and the other domestics, of course, and saying goodbye to them all brought up a rush of emotions that spilled out in tears and in bitter feelings about leaving. I continued to blame Mom for forcing Dad to take the general manager position, though I knew Dad was happy about it. But Mom was a convenient scapegoat. Her only saving grace was she insisted on Conceicão coming with us. And we did get to take our two cats, Mommy Kitty and Midnight, along with Conceicão's cat.

The hardest goodbye, of course, was to Zenia.

My mom drove me to Zenia's house the afternoon before we were to leave. Zenia's mom had made a *brigadeiro* cake, a rich, fudgy, four-layer cake; she cut us each a generous portion of the cake and we sat at their kitchen table, nibbling the cake while not saying much at the beginning. I think we didn't know how to say goodbye, and didn't want to say it, but didn't know what else to talk about. So, we sat there, eating the cake, while the two mothers chatted quietly a little ways away from us. Finally, Zenia spoke up.

"I'm going to miss you!" she said, her eyes sad.

Those words opened a floodgate of tears within me. Tears streaming down my face, I managed to croak, "I'm going to miss you, too!"

As good as the cake was—and everyone should have at least one slice of *brigadeiro* cake before they die—I was no longer hungry. I was too busy recalling the fun times we'd had together, and, with an eleven-year-old's mindset, thinking how cruel the world was to tear us apart.

"Now, girls, do not be so sad," Zenia's mother said, coming over to the table. "You know that your grandfather is a foreman at Bartira," she said to Zenia. Her mom smiled at me. "And we will come to visit. In fact, now we have *two* reasons to visit Bartira: Zenia's grandfather, and you!"

"Will you really come to visit?" I said to her mom.

"Of course we will! Now, do not let that good cake go to waste! Eat up, girls!"

That made us feel a little better. So, we finished our cake, and talked about different memories of sleepovers and playing together, and then we hugged and said goodbye. Mom made sure it was a quick goodbye, for my sake, hustling me out to the car so the sadness didn't have time to build.

"Don't worry," she said on the way home. "You'll keep in touch."

I just nodded, sulkily, and looked out the window at the houses in the colony; we passed some children who were gleefully screaming as they played tag. I thought how lucky they were to not be moving tomorrow.

"She's been a good friend to you, hasn't she?" Mom said.

I nodded again. I didn't even want to talk to Mom, because, as I said, she was playing the role of scapegoat in my life at the moment.

But I thought about her words as we traveled the dirt road back to Mosquito. Reluctantly, I had to agree with my mother.

Zenia was, in fact, both my first friend and my best friend in Brazil, and she made me feel so comfortable and welcome and at home in her native country. She helped me feel like a Brazilian, like someone who belonged, and for that, I would be forever grateful.

I will admit, looking back, that preadolescent girls can have a flair for the dramatic, emphasizing words like *never* and *always* in their speech and drawing emotions from an ever-deepening well within them (thanks to the hormones that are taking over their physical and emotional development). So, even though Zenia's mom promised to visit us at Bartira, that night, in bed, I cried myself to sleep as I figured I would *never* see my best friend again, and that I would *always* hate the fact that Mom—in my opinion—forced Dad to take the general manager position. (And I will also admit that preadolescents can be wrong: Zenia and I did stay in touch. I went back to Mosquito several times, and she visited Bartira many times when her family came to see her grandfather.)

The next day, I was a mix of emotions. I was sad and grumpy about leaving Mosquito, the ranch I'd lived on since I was four—and therefore the first place I had any significant memories of—but I also had some growing curiosity and excitement about heading to our next home. I had reconciled myself to the move, and gradually forced myself to look forward to what was next, not backward to what I was leaving behind.

During the two-hour trip Bartira, Jimmy and I began to pester our parents with questions: Was the house bigger than the Mosquito house? How many rooms did it have? How many people lived in the colonies? Were there kids our age? Were there good places to play? What towns was it near? It's safe to say we drove our parents crazy—which I took a delicious delight in, at least concerning Mom.

"Children! Can you just stop with the questions? You'll find out soon enough!" Mom finally said from the front seat after answering endless queries. Dad said nothing, but I do believe he drove a bit faster the rest of the way.

As we neared Bartira, we passed the machine shed, which was an open pole barn with sliding doors that could be locked at night. (The shed, we soon learned, was an excessively loud place with men seemingly always working on combines, tractors, pumps, and motors during the day. Jimmy and I, on many an evening, would throw stones on the shed's tin roof, listening to them clatter all the way down.) Then we drove by the horse corral, the single men's dormitory, and the camp house. The main office complex was near the corral; this was the head office for all five ranches. Continuing on this road, we passed three houses, the first belonging to Zenia's grandfather, as the head cowboy or foreman, the second to the head bookkeeper and his family, and the third being the Bartira manager's house, which is the house we had lived in when Jimmy was born. Farther down the road, which was lined with trees that would bloom annually with bright yellow flowers, we passed the soccer field and ended up at *sede nova* (new headquarters, or new house, which was built after the original manager's house), where we would live. Not far from the house was an airstrip with a hangar where the company plane was kept. Another road led from the soccer field through the pastures to the sawmill and on to Brasilandia, another Swift-King ranch ten miles west of Bartira.

Bartira had three housing units—an upper colony, middle colony, and lower colony. The upper colony was a row of three-bedroom brick duplex houses with running water and bathrooms, and the middle and lower colonies consisted of wooden two-bedroom houses with outhouses. All told, there were about forty families on the ranch.

"Here we are, kids!" Mom said as we pulled up to our house, her voice tinged with excitement. "Our new home!"

Jimmy, Theresa, and Michael were all pretty happy about the move; they saw it as a big adventure. They piled out of the car and raced into the house to check it out. I knew Jimmy was going to claim the best bedroom, but I didn't care where I slept. Let him have it.

"You're going to really like it here, honey," Mom said, putting her arm around my shoulder as we walked up the steps to the porch. I gave her a sullen look and said nothing.

"Mm, smell these flowers," Mom said as she sniffed some red and yellow blooms on a tropical vine on the porch screen. Though I secretly wanted to, I refused to smell them, not wanting to give the impression I liked anything about the house or the move.

Inside, it was smaller and darker than Mosquito. Two sliding doors led from the living room to the porch. They were almost always open because they were next to impossible to close. I would watch Candido struggle with those doors for the next three years, cursing them under his breath as he strained to shut them (or, on the rare occasion they were shut, to open them). Part of the difficulty was they had been painted over about a thousand times, or so it seemed. So this was our big step up?

We decorated the place with our own stuff, including the made-to-look-antique desk that Mom had put together herself from a purchase in Presidente Prudente and the mahogany bookcase that housed our *Encyclopedia Britannicas*, which my parents had bought back in Kingsville, Texas, from the salesman who wandered up to their street party. Another bookcase was filled with books leftover by guests. My personal favorite on those shelves was *The Joy of Sex,* which Mom used to explain what "getting my period" meant (and which Jimmy referred to as my "being on the rag" again). I thumbed through *The Joy of Sex* quite often on my own, enjoying the diagrams and descriptions of various body parts and sexual pleasures.

Pete, Jimmy, Betinha, Fazenda Mosquito. Author collection.

The house had a courtyard, where we were sometimes served dinner by Candido; a pool; an orchard with rows of various types of fruit trees: orange, grapefruit, mango, tangerine; and stepping stones that led to a guest house. Mom had the stones installed because guests would often slip and fall down the muddy incline to our house during the rainy season.

In our front yard we had a very cool round wooden table made from a tree trunk. Eight people could sit around it, and during the evenings in the dry season, Candido would set deck chairs around the table and my parents would sit at the table under the bright night sky with their nightcaps and their cigarettes. Sometimes we would join them, and sometimes a guest would point out certain planets and star formations. We loved it out there and would keep our eyes peeled for falling stars.

Bartira was only about twenty minutes from Rancharia, which had a movie theater and other amenities that were not readily available anywhere near Mosquito.

But I didn't care about any of this. I sulked for about three days, missing Zenia and my other friends, missing Mosquito and the maids there, missing the life I had been comfortable in and become accustomed to. After three days, my mother told me to snap out of it and make the most of what was in front of me rather than yearning for what was behind me.

Patience and consolation were not two of my mom's greatest strengths.

On the plus side, we did inherit a number of animals from Ed Lasater, who had recently been living on the ranch. Ed, in his hurry to return to Texas (or his total disdain for the animals), left behind a menagerie, including two dogs (a German Shepherd and a dachshund), two peafowl, two canaries, and several blue and yellow macaws.

On the minus side, many of these left-behind animals never endeared themselves to us, and I'm pretty sure my dad sent a few curse words toward Texas when he had to deal with the peafowl, which would roost on his car as if they owned it, and refused to move until Dad took a broom to them and helped them find the motivation to move. The peahen never managed to hatch the eggs she had laid, and the peacock, perhaps angered about not seeing any little peachicks scampering around, grew quite mean and took to chasing us bipeds whenever we wandered into his territory, which he considered to be wherever he happened to be at the moment. A few years after we moved in, the peafowl died, and we were free to roam about our yard again without fear of attack from the peacock and without having to hear it screech and scream during mating season. Believe me, no one mourned the birds when they died.

The macaws, too, died off, one by one, though one's demise was hastened by the dachshund, which, though little, was inch for inch as mean as the peacock. Jimmy and I joked that the macaw was taken from us by the "Jaws of Death," also known as the little yapping nuisance that puttered around the yard on its stubby legs.

And then there were the fighting cocks that Jimmy came up with from who knows where. He thought it would be cool to have fighting cocks, and they raised an awful ruckus when they fought. The beginning, middle, and end of their demise happened one morning when Mom came across six dead hens that had been torn apart by the cocks. Our tacos that evening tasted a bit gamey, but the remaining hen population clucked a bit less fearfully after that.

While the move to Bartira was hardly a good one for me, I have to admit—at least looking back now—that it was the right move for my dad. When he became general manager for all five Swift-King ranches in Brazil in 1969, the ranches, comprising 144,000 acres, had 23,000 head of cattle, 7,000 of them the Santa Gertrudis produced from the breeding program that my father was brought in to manage in the first place. (By the time my parents left Bartira, the herd had increased to

Pete Emmert and Jacque Fleming in front of General Manager house Fazenda Bartira, 1969. Mr. Fleming was a cattle buyer for Swift. Author collection.

40,000 cattle, with a breeding herd of 12,000, about 1,600 of which were purebred Santa Gertrudis cattle.) It was during our time at Bartira that Dad perfected the breeding program, finding the sweet spot between the tall rangy cows (common in Brazil) and the more compact, faster gaining animal (typical of US cattle). Dad bred cattle that fell in between these two extremes, and the results served the Swift-King operation very well.

He also succeeded in two other major projects. The first was breeding purebred quarter horses, which blossomed from its humble beginnings of one stallion and seven purebreds to over two hundred purebred and crossbred quarter horses, whose offspring became the most sought-after horses of this new breed in Brazil. The second project was putting all the land owned by Swift-King into good use—twelve thousand acres in crops and the rest in healthy pasture—not an easy feat to pull off in a tropical environment.

Another note of accomplishment: my parents were instrumental in bringing *leilões* (auctions) to the state of São Paulo. The first *leilão* was held in spring of 1968 at Bartira, and the following year a national association for quarter horse riders was formed. At that first *leilão,* both Santa Gertrudis cattle and quarter horses were auctioned, and soon these auctions were drawing people from as far north as Venezuela and as far south as Paraguay and Argentina. Upwards of five hundred people would attend these annual events, and of course they would be well fed with the finest barbecued beef in Brazil, along with side dishes and plenty of cold beer to keep even the thirstiest cowboys happy.

Mom was in charge of the food and entertainment for these *leilões,* and she was perfectly in her element as she orchestrated not only the barbecues for the day, but the buffet dinners for a select guest list of two hundred or so who were fed at our house and who then wandered out to dance under the stars. As I think back on it now, I am even more amazed at how my mother pulled all this off: no catering, no pre-bought food, no event planner (other than herself), no easy trips into town to get more of this or that. Just one woman in charge of a staff and planning food and entertainment for about five hundred people.

Say what you want about my mother—and people, including her children, said plenty about her, both good and bad—but she was an amazing and gifted woman who could do pretty much anything she put her mind to. We kids always said she could run a small country.

CHAPTER 8

LIFE AT BARTIRA

AS OUR FATHER GOT TO WORK AT BARTIRA in his new position as general manager of all five ranches, we kids settled into our school routine. Mom homeschooled Jimmy and me in a room in the three-bedroom, three-bathroom guest house. It was a nicely designed house, very modern, and furnished in good taste. The porch, accessed from either end of the living room by sliding glass doors, was often used for dance parties. But for Jimmy and me, the guest house signified school time.

Which, all things considered, was okay with us, because Theresa and Michael, being younger, were tutored by Mrs. Murray in a one-room building behind the maids' quarters. She and her son Gary had come with us to Bartira (Gary's dad was moving back to the States, and Mom and Dad told Mrs. Murray it would be fine for Gary to live with her on the ranch). Jimmy and I were quite happy to never be placed under Mrs. Murray's tutelage.

Looking back, I feel sorry for Gary. He was a year older than me, but he—like his mother—stood out from his peers. He didn't fit in with us; he was a serious, quiet kid, a bit of a "goody two shoes" in our opinion, and I have to admit that Jimmy and I picked on him pretty frequently. We called him a mama's boy, we'd let the air out of his bicycle tires, and we teased him mercilessly while he sat around reading books. One afternoon, I am ashamed to admit now, we threw bricks at him, which of course landed us in hot water with our parents.

Not long after that, Mom called us four kids into the living room.

"Sit down," she said, and we sat, two on the couch, two on chairs.

"I didn't do it," Jimmy said with a slightly guilty look on his face.

"Do what?" Mom said. "I didn't say you did anything."

"Oh."

I could tell Jimmy wished he hadn't spoken up, and I giggled.

"Yeah, what didn't you do, Jimmy?" I teased. "Tell us what you didn't do."

"I didn't do anything!" Jimmy retorted.

"I'll bet you did—"

"Children! Stop it! No one's in trouble here." She arched her eyebrow at Jimmy. "No matter what anyone did or didn't do, I wanted to let you know that Mrs. Murray and Gary are leaving. They are headed back to the US."

Looks of excitement and glee crossed our faces. I started to clap for joy, but a dark look from my mother stopped me in mid-clap.

"Enough of that! I want you all to go wish them well. And I want you to mean it. Try being kind to them for once. And Theresa and Michael, I want you to make thank-you cards for Mrs. Murray." Apparently, Jimmy and I avoided this onerous task because we weren't tutored by her.

Jimmy and I glanced at each other. We figured we could tell a little white lie to Mrs. Murray and Gary if that meant we didn't have to see them again. So, the next morning, as they were getting ready to take the bus to São Paulo for their flight, we wished them well. We didn't have any trouble smiling, because we were happy to see them leave.

And so Mrs. Murray, who had stormed abruptly into our lives four years earlier, made nearly as unexpected an exit.

"Goodbye, Mrs. Murray," I said, waving as the car pulled away.

"Good riddance, you old bat," Jimmy said, not realizing Mom was within hearing distance.

"Jimmy! You want me to wash your mouth out with soap?" Mom said.

"Oh! No, sorry. I was just joking."

"So what was it that you swear you 'didn't do,' anyway?" Mom asked.

"Nothing! I already told you, I didn't do anything!"

That was probably a bigger lie than the one he just told Mrs. Murray when he wished her well. Jimmy was always up to *something*.

But then again, so was his big sister. I seemed to excel at getting into trouble in a great variety of ways as I grew older. (Not that getting into trouble was anything new for me. For example, at Mosquito we had an assistant manager named Allan. He and some other men were planting shade trees in the yard. For some reason I thought it would be funny to kick sand and dirt back in the holes the men were digging. Allan told me to stop—several times. I took his command as a challenge, and continued kicking sand and dirt in the holes when he turned back to his work. Eventually he dropped his shovel and spanked me. Allan told my mother what had happened, and I got a second spanking. After Allan, we had another assistant manager, this one named Eric. One early evening Eric was on the porch, reading, and I was playing with blocks—that's how young I was. I thought, this is fun, but it would be more fun to throw some blocks at Eric. So I threw some blocks at him; they bounced off his legs. He told me to stop. Which I did, until he looked back at his magazine. Then I threw some more blocks—one of which hit him in the eye. Eric got up and spanked me, and ratted me out to Mom, who repeated the spanking. All along I was sure it was Eric who was going to get in trouble for having the audacity to spank me. No such luck.)

At Bartira, a man named Altino worked in the office. He was a nice guy, always in a good mood, always joking around. He liked to gab and would talk your ear off if you let him. He was one of those guys you liked to be around because he always lifted your mood.

If Altino had had access to it back then, he would have been a subscriber to the *National Enquirer*. He loved gossip, was entranced by the legends of Bigfoot and the Loch Ness Monster, and was always on the lookout for aliens. And, we found out, he was ever so gullible.

So, imagine the look on my father's face when, on the day before some guests were arriving to visit him on the ranch, Altino told my father it would be so exciting if the flying saucers would appear again so his guests could see them.

"The *what*?" my dad said.

"The *discos voadores*," Altino said. "They have been appearing at night on holidays. Between my house and Candido's. You have not seen them?"

"Um . . . no. I haven't seen them, Altino."

"Watch for them! They usually appear around 9 p.m.! I hope they will show up tomorrow. We should get a picture to send to the paper, don't you think?"

"Sure. If you see any flying saucers, take a picture. Good idea."

Altino thanked him and went on his way. My father, meanwhile, tracked Jimmy and me down.

"Seems flying saucers have been appearing on holidays between Altino's house and Candido's house. Have you seen them?" he asked us, already knowing the answer—and who was behind the appearance of the "saucers."

"Oh, wow!" Jimmy said. "Flying saucers?"

"Right here, right over our ranch?" I chimed in.

"Yes. Odd, don't you think?" my father said.

"Very odd," I said, but I couldn't stop a giggle from coming out. I snuck a look at Jimmy and he started guffawing. Pretty soon we were both doubled over in laughter.

"Altino seems to think they will appear again tomorrow night. What do you think?" Dad said.

"I don't know," Jimmy said, nearly breathless as he wiped tears of laughter from his cheeks. "That depends on if we have fresh batteries in the house."

We divulged our method of creating *discos voadores:* varying lengths of rope, varying sizes of flashlights, and varying vantage points in the large meadow between Altino's and Candido's houses. We'd attach the flashlights to the ropes and start swinging them overhead while on horseback, clipping along at a nice pace to give the impression that the flying saucers were taking off and landing. Michael and Theresa would help us, and we would have four UFOs circling the meadow.

After telling Dad this, he laughed long and hard—but he also told us to go down to the office and explain to Altino what we had done.

"Do we have to?" Jimmy said.

"Yes, you have to."

So we went down to the office and told Altino what we had been doing and apologized.

"So, no *discos voadores?*" he said, a sad look on his face.

"No *discos voadores,*" I said.

He looked very disappointed. He had been so excited to show his friends the flying saucers. We went away still thinking the hoax was pretty clever and funny, but feeling a little bad for fooling this nice man.

Jimmy, being closest in age to me, was often my fellow prankster-in-arms. One time he and I decided to soap a couple of cars outside the manager's house during a dinner party at Bartira. Under cover of night, we went to work with a bucket of water, some soap, and a flashlight (they proved useful for more than creating flying saucers), and then hid in the bushes, waiting for our victims to discover the prank.

The two couples, Marcel and Charlotte Gros, who ran Brasilandia Ranch, and Ed and Linda Cope, who were the local managers on Bartira Ranch, finally emerged from our house and walked to their cars. To see the flustered dismay on their faces was, as the old MasterCard commercials would say, priceless. We had to cover our mouths to keep from laughing out loud and being caught.

Mr. Cope, however, failed to see the humor in the soaping.

"I saw Pete's two older kids skulking around here earlier," he said to his wife and the Groses. "I know it was them." He told the Groses he was going back to our house to tell Dad the fiendish thing we had done. The Groses actually thought it was sort of funny, so we thought we were okay with them.

Jimmy and I hightailed it home, running through the soccer field and the "*discos voadores*" field. We ran up, breathless, to our back door, figuring Mr. Cope would come to the front door. Once we could breathe normally, we walked inside, our plan being to be seen with Mom as soon as possible ("How could we have done it? We were here sitting and talking to Mom").

Oddly, Mr. Cope didn't show up that night. We learned later that Charlotte Gros had talked him out of complaining about the soaping.

However, the next morning, the two couples showed up at our house, asking, tongue-in-cheek, if they could have their cars washed, as they had heard that we provided such services.

Some of our shenanigans nearly backfired on us, though. When I was twelve, Jimmy and I begged Jimmy Herbert, who was over eighteen and thus legal to drive, to let us crawl onto the hood of Dad's company car and the top of the trunk while he drove. (His parents, Francis and Martha Herbert, were former managers at Bartira who lived in São Paulo. Francis, who was president of Swift-King and also of Swift Packers in Brazil, was Dad's boss.)

Jimmy Herbert thought that was a grand idea, so my brother and I climbed onto his car and Jimmy Herbert floored it down a dirt road, a cloud of dust rising in the air behind us. Jimmy and I were laughing and screaming (half in fun, half in fear). Once I nearly fell off, my hands burning from hanging on, my fingers feeling like they were going to break or simply have to let go of the rather precarious hold I had on the hood. Another time, Daniel, Jimmy Herbert's brother, and I were on the hood, hanging on together, and when Jimmy Herbert turned a corner, we both slid off and rolled and tumbled into the ditch beside the road. Jimmy Herbert became very upset—I'm sure he was scared that we were badly hurt, and we did have plenty of scrapes and bruises, but nothing serious—and he said he was never doing that again. Then he drove off, leaving us to walk back to the house, which was a good mile away.

I never argued with Jimmy Herbert about letting us pull that stunt again. Falling off once was more than enough for me.

And then there were the times I got in trouble even when I wasn't intentionally doing anything to cause it. Like the time when I was twelve or thirteen and the Gelds were coming for a fun summer weekend—weekend guests were always cause for great excitement in our house—and I decided we should paint flowers and designs on the inner tubes for our pool. I gathered up three partially-used paint cans, some paint brushes, and an inner tube in my arms and walked through our kitchen and into the dining room, where Mom was sitting, writing Christmas cards. The can handles were cutting into my fingertips and I was beginning to lose my grip on them. Hindsight being 20/20, it's possible I shouldn't have carried so many cans and an inner tube through our house.

"Hey Mom, can I—"

At that point the pressure on my fingers was too great, and a can of oil-based white paint—whose lid, I was soon to discover, was not tightly secured—fell to the floor and toppled over, spilling onto the parquet floor and flowing onto the sisal rug under the dining room table.

"Betinha! Oh my gosh! Look what you did!" She slapped me across the face and told me to get out. I don't think I had ever seen her so angry, and I was frightened. I began crying as I ran out of the house. I didn't think I deserved that slap, which was still stinging, or that anger from her. I hid in the garden, rubbing my cheek, afraid to return to the house.

Theresa and Michael came up at one point, hours later, and asked what I was doing. I thought it was quite clear what I was doing: I was sitting with my back to a tree, crying. And thinking evil thoughts about Mom.

"Why are you crying?" Theresa asked.

"None of your business! Just go away."

"Did you get in trouble?" Michael asked.

"No! Just leave me alone."

Jimmy came up and said Mom and Dad were talking in the living room. Mom was still livid, apparently. He told Theresa and Michael about the paint on the floor, and their eyes grew big.

"Oh my gosh, she's going to skin you alive!" Theresa said.

"Thanks for that," I said sarcastically.

Jimmy's report got the best of me, and I decided to creep back into the house and try to hear their conversation. I wanted to know if Dad was calming her down or if I needed to pack some bags and hit the road.

Mrs. Murray, who was still with us at the time, had a bathroom that shared a wall with the dining room, so I hid in her shower and listened in.

"I don't know where she is!" Mom was saying. "She's been gone for hours."

"You scared her off," Dad said. "You shouldn't have been so harsh on her."

"I wasn't harsh! But what do you expect, that I would thank her for spilling paint on the floor?"

"No, but—"

"She's going to get the spanking of her life when I find her," Mom muttered.

"Ease off. Look, Candido cleaned up the paint anyway. It was just an accident."

"She didn't even say she was sorry!"

Because you didn't give me a chance, I thought.

I returned to the garden and stayed hidden for a few more hours, and by that time, Mom's temper had cooled enough and the worry instinct that all mothers have when their children are missing kicked in. Jimmy let me know that she was no longer looking to tan my hide, but just wanted me home, and I came back to the house.

In fact, things had calmed down enough that I still painted the flowers and designs on the inner tubes. But I wished I had never thought of the idea—or had gone to ask Mom about it *without* the paint cans in hand!

When Mrs. Murray and Gary returned to the US, we hired a woman named Diana Sheely to be Theresa and Michael's tutor. Diana was the daughter of John and Weenie Sheely; her dad came from the US and was a local manager at Bartira. Her mom was from an Argentine family who owned the largest shipping line in Santos, Brazil. Diana was fluent in English, Spanish, and Portuguese; after her tutoring sessions were finished for the day, she taught English lessons in Rancharia.

Diana was friendly and kind, and I remember being mesmerized as I sat and watched her put her makeup on in her bathroom as she got ready for the day. Diana was in her late twenties and was a bit of a role model for me—someone who was older, but not so ancient as my parents. She loved getting all made up and wearing jewelry, and she looked elegant when she got dressed up to go out for an evening.

I did have a couple of embarrassing moments (naturally) with Diana. One was when she took me into Rancharia to watch the movie *Romeo & Juliet*; I cried my eyes out at the unfair fate of these two young lovers but felt silly doing so in front of her. The second "I wish this hadn't happened" moment was when she had her boyfriend over and the Renwick girls, Karleen and Heather, and I decided to go skinny-dipping at night. (We were eleven and twelve years old.) It was just silly fun, but it turned into red-faced embarrassment when we ran from the pool back to the house, only to be seen by Diana and her boyfriend, who were standing outside by a door. We scurried behind the barbecue pit to hide, and later made Diana promise not to tell our parents.

"Fine, but no more skinny-dipping!" she said. "At least not when my boyfriend is around."

Diana was with us for two years before she got married (not to the young man who had seen us in our birthday suits, but to someone else), and they moved to Santos, a coastal city not far from São Paulo. Our next—and last—tutor was Tammy, an American who had graduated from college and come to live with her parents in São Paulo after her father had been transferred there for work.

Tammy was a step down from Diana, in my opinion. She came off as a know-it-all (though she knew no Portuguese), and she didn't have the charm, grace, or beauty that Diana possessed. Looking back, I feel bad for Tammy, because she seemed lonely and always had to hear her parents gush over her sister, who was more attractive, more successful, and married. She tagged along with us kids everywhere we went, and didn't leave the ranch unless it was with us. I considered her more of a friend than anything (she didn't tutor me except on days Mom was gone, though I hated those days because Tammy went into "strict teacher" mode and drove me crazy). She taught me how to needlepoint and we had fun talking and riding horses together. We would ride every morning before school, and she would do figure eights with her horse on the soccer field. She taught us how to jump, and though quarter horses aren't the best at jumping, we had a lot of fun doing that (except for the times the horses would stop short and we would fly off).

Mom promised me that when I turned thirteen, I could get my ears pierced. Which only put me about thirteen years behind Brazilian girls, most of whom had their ears pierced at birth. But I was ecstatic and couldn't wait for the day to arrive. When it finally did, I opened my presents, chief among them being gold ball earrings from my parents. I shrieked, hugged them both, and ran down to the office, surprising

Altino, our assistant bookkeeper (the one whom Jimmy and I duped into believing flying saucers were near the ranch). Altino was the closest thing to a nurse we had on the ranch.

"Altino! Can you do me a big favor?" I asked, out of breath from both my running and my excitement.

"What is it? What's wrong?"

"Nothing's wrong! I got these for my birthday, and I need someone to pierce my ears!" I showed him the earrings, and he oohed appreciatively.

"Can you do it?" I asked him.

"Well, I have nothing but the earring stud to do it with."

"That's fine! Just do it!"

"Maybe you should go into town and—"

"No! I want them in now. You can do it. Just use the studs."

He sighed. "Okay. It might hurt a little."

I didn't care. I normally didn't have the highest threshold for pain—but normally my first set of earrings was not the object producing the pain, either.

So, Altino sanitized the studs and my earlobes and went about the business of poking holes in my ears, using one of the posts from an old earring of Mom's to pierce my lobes. To be honest, I felt no pain—I think I was too ecstatic about getting earrings, which I had wanted for three or four years. *Finally,* I would be like all the Brazilian girls who wore earrings every day. I felt suddenly *sophisticated* and older.

Having earrings on made going into Rancharia for my guitar lessons—Mom insisted Jimmy and I learn the guitar, as the piano hadn't stuck with us—more tolerable, as I would ask Amadeus to give our head accountant Senhor Paulo's daughter Nanci and me some time to walk up and down some streets in Rancharia, flirting with the boys we passed by.

By this time, I was keenly interested in boys, and I asked (okay, nagged) my mother to buy me a pair of high-heeled shoes, but she said no way. So, naturally, I went to Plan B, also known as Dad, who said, "Are you sure it's okay with your mother?"

"Why not?" I said, shrugging and looking innocent.

So, he and I went to town and I picked out a pair of three-inch red-and-black heels.

"You've got to be kidding me," Dad said as I tried the shoes on in the store.

"What?"

"*That's* the fashion nowadays?"

"What's wrong with them?" I began walking up and down the aisle on them. I couldn't believe how much taller—and older—I felt.

"How about what's *right* with them? That'd be a much shorter answer."

"I like them," I said, turning my foot this way and that as I peered at the shoes in a mirror.

"You'll fall and twist your ankle. Or get arrested for wearing shoes too ugly for public viewing. One or the other."

I *was* having a bit of a time trying to get used to walking in the heels, but I figured I'd get used to them soon. I took care not to walk too much more in them while he was watching, and focused on wheedling him enough to get him to buy me the shoes. I could tell it was against his better judgment, but he paid for them, and we walked out of the shoe store—me a few paces behind, proudly strutting down the cobblestone street in my new heels, out of his view so he couldn't see how clumsy I was in them. (Believe me, cobblestone streets are *not* the ideal surface on which to learn how to walk in heels!)

When we got home, Mom was none too pleased.

"Why did you buy her those godawful things?" she said to Dad.

"She told me you were okay with it," he said.

"I never said she was okay with it," I hastily said, eyeing my mother to gauge her anger level, which was merely on simmer. I just said 'Why not?' when you asked me."

Oh, the trickery and deceit a thirteen-year-old will stoop to to get her first pair of heels.

I never did twist my ankle in them, by the way—but I do have to agree with Dad now. They *were* butt ugly.

If there ever was a dysfunctional family as far as driving is concerned, it was ours. Dad hated to drive but was the one who taught me how (at age thirteen). Mom loved to drive but would regularly run out of gas. I loved to drive, too, but was—despite my Dad's best efforts—not the best at it, at least starting out.

My dad's method of teaching was trial by fire. He'd come by the house after school and tell me to hop in his company car. (My mother had warned him "If you let her practice in my car, I might actually kill you.") I was thrilled to be behind the wheel. Thirteen was a big year for me: pierced ears, high heels, and now driving. I was allowed to drive on the ranch, which was quite huge.

I found I showed immediate aptitude for grinding the gears on the stick shift; only Mom's car was an automatic. So, I would shift (grind), shift (grind), causing my dad to grimace, or laugh as he instructed me how to smoothly shift, or both.

Anyway, my dad would have me start the car and take off down the road, and then had me turn down the dirt road toward the mill. This road was very sandy, and when it rained, the dirt and the sand became a quagmire where the land dipped into a little valley. One day I drove down this road after a recent rain and, not knowing how to get through the quagmire, I got us stuck. Trying to go either forward or backward, the tires just spun and sprayed mud and sand behind us. Revving the engine to try to get some traction just made the engine whine and me panic.

I looked over at him. "What do I do?" I said, my heart fluttering in my chest.

He looked over at me casually and said, "Now you walk."

"What?"

"You walk. Go back to the shop and find Mr. Ziller. Tell him we need a tractor out here to rescue us."

"But that's like a mile back!"

"Better get going then."

"Dad! Can't you get us out?"

"Sure. Once a tractor comes." I noticed then that he had brought paperwork with him. He was expecting this to happen, which only made me madder.

"But I'm wearing *flip-flops*!" I said, hoping he would have pity on me.

"Guess you'll have to hose them and your feet off."

I grumbled and complained some more, but he said if the driver got the car in trouble in the first place, it was the driver's responsibility to get it out of trouble.

"And next time, don't slow down when you come to that spot. Shift into a lower gear, and pick up some momentum and drive right through it like you mean it."

Another time, Mom was driving with Dad and Beatrice Olivera, a friend of theirs who was married to one of the ranch managers. They were headed to São Paulo. Dad had told Mom to be sure to gas the car up before they left. Sure enough, they ran out of gas on the highway to Rancharia, about a mile from a little village that did have a gas station.

(Beatrice, by the way, was one of what was called the *Quatrocentaos,* or "the four hundred"; the *Quatrocentaos* were the elite families in Brazil whose ancestors came from Portugal to São Paulo in the 1800s, when Portugal was invaded by French troops. To be a *Quatrocentaos* was like being royalty in Brazil. And she married well, too: her husband, Marcio, was an Olympian, having competed in the 1936 Berlin Olympics. Marcio was a cattle buyer for Swift and a manager of one of the ranches when this incident happened.)

"I can't believe this!" Mom said, slamming her palm on the steering wheel and muttering a few choice curses under her breath to drive home the point that she couldn't believe it.

"I can," Dad said calmly, while taking in the scenery around them.

"What happened?" Beatrice asked from the back seat. When Mom told her, she said, "Oh, that's too bad!" and looked at Dad, who was still enjoying the scenery, whistling a little tune.

"Pete? Aren't you going to do something?" Beatrice said.

He twisted around to face Mom's friend and said with a big smile, "I'm already doing it, Beatrice."

Beatrice's jaw dropped as Dad continued to sit and Mom got out of the car and started walking.

"Should be about a mile up the road," he hollered. "Can't miss it."

"I know, I know," Mom called back over her shoulder, waving her hand in dismissal at him without even turning around.

"Why aren't you going to get the gas?" Beatrice demanded. She was flabbergasted that Dad would let Mom walk a mile to a gas station. And back, hopefully.

"Because I'm not the one who ran out of gas," Dad said cheerfully. "Besides, it'll do her good. Stretch her legs out a little."

Beatrice let out a humph from the back seat while Dad settled down a bit in his seat, closed his eyes, and napped.

With Dad, you do things right, you take care of your responsibilities, or you learn your lesson. The hard way.

Life at Bartira also involved, as you can imagine, lots of animals. Sometimes it felt like I lived in a zoo—dogs, cats, parrots, monkeys, and of course horses and cattle.

And the occasional (and unwanted) bee. Such as the time that Candido's brother, Paulinho, who worked in the machine shop and lived in the upper colony, grudgingly allowed Billy Herbert and me to accompany Jimmy and him to the beehives to collect honey. Jimmy often went with Paulinho to the hives, but this would be the first time for me. I think I was partly bored, partly curious, and partly jealous that Jimmy always got to go.

"Fine, you can come," Paulinho said one summer evening as the sun was dipping below the horizon. "But I want you to be quiet and not be bouncing around and disturbing the bees."

Billy and I eagerly nodded our heads. "You got it!" I said. And I meant it. I didn't want to disturb any bees, believe me. I just wanted to see the process; there was something alluring about watching someone stick his arm into a wild beehive, with hundreds of bees buzzing around and crawling on his flesh.

The hive, hanging from one of the dead trees that were left standing after the land was cleared, looked massive and ominous as we approached it in the dusk. (Thankfully, *The Swarm*, a horror movie about a killer bee invasion in Texas, was seven years away from hitting the theaters. Had I seen that movie, I would not have been begging Paulinho to let me go with him.) Paulinho and Jimmy approached the hive, Jimmy a step behind. Billy and I were a few steps behind Jimmy.

"What if they swarm out and attack us?" I said rather nervously.

"Then Senhor Paulinho and Billy and I don't have to worry," Jimmy said. "Bees only go after girls if they're around."

"That's not true," I said, but Paulinho hushed us and I was left wondering if it *were* true. I gulped and took a step back.

Paulinho slowly reached his arm into the hive, and in the dim light it looked like his arm became twice as thick as it was, with thousands of bees crawling on it (in reality it was probably dozens, but it seemed like thousands at the time). I screamed, Jimmy told me to shut up, Billy started shouting and running around, and the bees, stirred by all the commotion, exited the hive and filled the air around us, buzzing and humming around our heads and bodies. My scream turned into a shriek as several flew into my hair and I could feel them vibrating in it. Billy was screaming, too, and was stung a few times, and Jimmy was shouting for us to shut up and quit running around like idiots, and Paulinho was angrily walking away from the hive, muttering to himself. Taking my cue from him, I ran from the hive, shaking my head and quickly running my hands through my hair to get rid of the bees, who probably wanted to be as free of me as I wanted to be free of them. I ran shrieking all the way to the house, and Mom ran up to find out what the ruckus was about, and Jimmy came up and said "Never again is she going with us to get the honey!" and I said "Don't worry, I don't plan on it!"

Paulinho, in addition to keeping bees, also liked to capture baby parrots. The chicks can be an adorable mix of homely and cute. The cowboys would alert Paulinho as to nest locations on the ranch, and he would go out at night to parrot-nap them. They would nest in dead trees or rotted trunks.

One evening, Paulinho brought back three baby parrots, and I fell in love with the largest of the litter—a skinny, featherless, homely looking creature with a huge curved beak and four very large toes at the end of each spindly leg, two toes pointing forward, two pointing back.

"Aw, he's so cute!" I said. "Can I have him?"

Paulinho rolled his eyes, but he grudgingly gave the bird to me, in part because he knew my dad wasn't keen on him taking the birds from their nest and selling them in the first place.

"Tell your dad you found this one at the bottom of a tree," he said. "You understand?"

I understood. His secret was good with me, so long as I got to keep Pepé, as I named my scrawny new pet.

Mom allowed me to keep Pepé in a dark box on the back porch (the darkness had a soothing effect on him). I fed him bread sopped in milk in a spoon, and he noisily slurped down his food and squawked when feeding time was over. After a few weeks, Pepé began to sprout little peach-fuzz white feathers; later he got his green feathers in. His vocal chords were also getting stronger as he got older, and my siblings and I decided it was time to teach Pepé how to speak. We kept repeating words and phrases for about a week, but Pepé seemed to only care about his food.

"How come he won't talk?" I asked Candido one day.

"Give him time, child," he said. "You didn't learn to talk overnight either." He gave me a tip: talk to the bird when its cage (we had him in a cage with a perch by this point) was covered with a towel, so it wouldn't be distracted.

So we used the towel method, and kept at it—and sure enough, as a few more weeks went by, Pepé started to talk! His first words were Portuguese cuss words, which didn't thrill Mom as much as it thrilled us kids.

"Cut the crap," Mom said to us in the kitchen one day. "No more cussing from that bird, you understand?"

"But *crap* is a cuss word, isn't it?" Michael asked innocently.

"Yeah, you're not supposed to say *crap*," Jimmy chimed in, aware that Pepé would sometimes repeat a word if he heard it enough times in a short span.

"Crap! Crap! Crap!" Pepé squawked, to our nearly unanimous utter delight. Mom groaned and walked out of the room, leaving us kids laughing and praising Pepé—once Mom was out of earshot.

Pepé also learned how to screech Michael's name in the middle of the night, which was fun for the whole household, and as he aged he became quite adept at mimicking the maids in the kitchen, even parroting their intonations. Everyone got a kick out of Pepé, but the bird itself highly favored Candido. Pepé would not perch on anyone else's finger except for Candido's. Pepé would not let anyone else touch him, but he would lean his head toward Candido as Candido gently rubbed his head feathers.

As for me, the rightful owner and master of the bird? I could get Pepé to perch on a broomstick that I held, but as soon as he started edging his way toward me with that sharp beak of his, I would put the broomstick down.

I guess you could say, based on the previous few pages, that I learned about the birds and the bees at Bartira. Along with many other creatures—including pigs.

When I was eleven years old, our family visited our good friends the Gelds, who were living in Tietê, about a seven-hour drive from Bartira. Carson and Ellen, my parents' best friends in Brazil, were a little on the wild side, as I've mentioned. (You remember Chico, their spider monkey, who perched on my head while eating my food?) But they were as wonderful as they were wacky. I always loved spending time with them, and endured the seven-hour drive for the reward of hanging out with their family for a while.

Anyway, during one visit to the Gelds' ranch in Tietê, Carson's prized sow gave birth to a litter of piglets. I happened to be with Carson when the sow began to birth the piglets.

"Is she really going to give birth today?" I asked as we leaned against a fence, watching the great sow as she lay on the wooden floor, breathing a bit heavier than normal. She was in a separate farrowing stall so she wouldn't be bothered during the process.

"Yep," Carson said. He pointed out the sow's teats—a dozen of them, all with droplets of milk on the tips. "That says she's ready," he said.

Just then, the sow's top hind leg shivered.

"And that means they're coming soon," he added. He said that sometimes a sow will twitch her tail shortly before giving birth as well.

I watched, fascinated, as the tip of a piglet's nose soon appeared from the birth canal. The head slowly emerged, but once the head was out, the shoulders and rest of the body slid out pretty quickly. The little piglet tried several times to stand, falling each time, but within a few minutes it was able to stand, and it wobbled over to feed from one of the teats. I was amazed that the sow didn't bellow and holler like the colony women did when they gave birth (Zenia and I had many times snuck around to a colony house where a woman was about to give birth, perching below the open bedroom window while a midwife would help the woman in her obvious agony).

The first piglet kept feeding and snuggling up against its mother as the sow kept about the business of farrowing. The piglets were born about fifteen minutes apart—nine of them all told—and I absolutely fell in love with the tiniest one, number eight, who had trouble finding his way to a teat. I had gone off to play with the Geld kids once Carson told me the births would be fifteen to twenty minutes apart and the sow might have ten or twelve piglets, but I had returned right as the eighth piglet slithered out into the world and struggled to find his way. Carson helped him get to a teat.

For some reason the name "Charlie" popped into my head as I watched this little guy have his first meal. He was reddish-brown and he looked perfect and sweet. The sow, after finishing, lay contentedly on her side for a bit, letting the litter feed.

"Oh, can I have him?" I blurted out.

"Can you *have* him?" Carson seemed surprised. I guess no one had ever asked him for a piglet before.

"Please? I'll take good care of him. I promise."

Carson considered this for a moment, then grinned. "Well, I can give it to you once it's weaned. So long as your parents are good with it," he said.

"Oh, they'll be fine with it!"

Guess what? They were *not* fine with it. A seven-hour ride home with a brand-new piglet was not, to their way of thinking, that great of an idea. In fact, it was an out-and-out *bad* idea, according to my mother, but Carson said it would teach me responsibility and some other attributes which I don't remember but readily agreed with back then. Concentrating on my father (I know Mom would not change her mind), I gave him my sad yet hopeful face with my innocent eyes. He hesitated, and I could see him crumbling by the second.

"All right, once it's weaned, we can take it home with us—if you promise to take care of it," he said. "Like Carson said, it's *your* responsibility."

"I will, I promise!" I said, and as Mom rolled her eyes and said "Oh my God!" I hugged Dad.

Before Charlie came to live with us, Dad had a few men build a pen in the orchard, and I spent a lot of time at his pen, talking to him and feeding him Purina hog chow mixed with kitchen slops.

Charlie was a Duroc pig, part of a breed developed to form the basis for many mixed-breed commercial hogs. He had adorable droopy ears, and he was a docile and most affable swine, pleasant-tempered and loving. He would nudge me, kiss me with his snout, cuddle with me, and sometimes even try to lick my face to show his affection.

As most Durocs do, Charlie grew quickly. When he was old enough to sire—at about thirty weeks—I bought a sow named Dolly. I'm sad to say that Dolly was not deserving of Charlie; she was ugly, ill-mannered, and several notches below Charlie's social status, in my estimation. But she did bear many piglets for Charlie, all of which we sold except for two males, which we castrated and kept to fatten.

Dolly, while nasty in every other way, *was* good at farrowing, and soon the idea came to me that I could use Charlie to provide stud services. Why not? Give Charlie a little fun and make some money while I was at it.

Charlie, in part because of his immense size—he eventually weighed in at 750 pounds—developed a reputation far and wide. Soon, farmers from all over, many at least twenty miles away, would bring their sows to the ranch to breed with Charlie. At times, there was a line of pickups near Charlie's pen. I'll never forget the afternoon that Dad came home and, seeing me at the kitchen table, said, "What's with all the pickups out by Charlie's pen?"

"That's my business," I said, airily.

"Don't take that tone with me, Betinha."

"No, I mean, that's my *business.* Literally. My stud boar service."

"Your *what*?"

"Charlie's got quite the reputation, Dad. Farmers from all over are coming with their sows." I grinned. "Not a bad little side business for me, eh?"

His jaw dropped. When it eventually hinged well enough for him to speak again, he said "Not bad at all. That's amazing. My little business girl." He smiled and walked out of the room, shaking his head.

I ran my stud boar business for about seven years, keeping it going with the help of our gardener when I was away at boarding school. I would pay the gardener for his work and still was making money hand over fist. When I went off to college, I turned over the operation to Michael. On my first visit home, I learned that Michael had quickly become bored with the work involved, had Charlie castrated, and sold him to a butcher. I was furious with Michael, as Charlie was *my* hog, and it took me a long time to get over it.

Later, as I thought about it, I understood even more clearly why Dad had been so upset with me a few years earlier for paying off the man whose car I had run into with meat from the ranch. That meat was not *my* property to barter with, just as Charlie was not *Michael's* property to dispense with.

Looking back on my time not only in Bartira, but in Brazil in general, I know that despite my great affection for Charlie, my favorite animals were the ever-present horses on the ranches.

On Saturdays I would wake up before Dad and put my saddle in his car and wait for him to finish breakfast and drive me to the corral. From there, I would saddle "my" horse (I saddled the same one each time, and considered him mine, but it was really a ranch horse) and ride with the cowboys as they checked on the cattle. They didn't mind me riding with them but didn't want too many "outsiders" (guests or friends of mine), most of whom didn't know horses or how to ride.

That didn't stop me from trying to show off for my friends and our guests. Theresa and I would practice standing on the horses' backs while they were cantering. (We also typically each tried to hit the other horse while doing this, or to untie the girth that was fastened around the horse's belly. We were probably lucky we didn't fall off and break our necks.)

Some of our cockier guests who swore they were great riders were given the opportunity to show their talents on horses that had never had a saddle before, or that had not been broken and, once started, could not be easily stopped. The cockiness from the riders' faces would soon give way to concern and, at times, terror, as their horse bolted away and they were left to hang on for dear life. More than once these rather egotistical riders were tossed by their horses, and most of them came back humbled and shaking.

Though I loved horses, I was only an average rider at best, and this was compounded by my refusal to ride with a saddle. Many times, when riding with the Emmerts or the Herberts, one of the boys would try to spook my horse, and once my horse bucked a bit and I slid off and fell. I acted like I was seriously hurt and then pretended to faint, and all the kids frantically carried me to our house and to my bed. As I was still in "fake faint" mode, I heard many of the boys swear they were never going to play this stupid game again, and how sorry they were, and how they hoped I wasn't seriously injured. What if I had broken my neck or my back? Maybe I would be paralyzed. Or maybe I landed on my head and sustained brain damage. They didn't know, but the possibilities just kept spilling out of their mouths until I couldn't stand it anymore and started cracking up.

"What the heck?" one of the Herbert boys said. "Have you been hearing our whole conversation?"

I made a big deal of easily and swiftly sitting up on my bed—obviously nothing was wrong with me. But then, laughing, I held the side of my neck, made it go crooked, and said, "Oh! I think my neck is broken!" And I fell back on the bed again, amidst shouts and curses from the boys.

I was pretty much *persona non grata* for the next twenty-four hours or so, but it was worth it. And even though I wasn't seriously injured, and the boys were ticked, it *had* taught them a lesson.

CHAPTER 9

"WE MANAGED TO SAVE THE BOOZE" AND OTHER RANCH STORIES

I HATED PLAYING PIANO.

I hated it even more after one rainy spring afternoon in May of 1967.

Mom thought I should play. It was part of her "We may live on a ranch, but we are *cultured* people" way of thinking. How we decorated our home, how we spoke, how we entertained, what our leisure pursuits were, all emanated from—at least for her—the desire to live an educated, refined, intellectually and artistically aware life that spoke of a certain level of sophistication. We lived in the country; indeed, we *made* our living *off* the country, but we were as far removed from country bumpkins as east is from west.

So, on this rainy Thursday afternoon, our driver, Aniba, drove me from Mosquito Ranch to Presidente Prudente, a torturous journey of forty miles—torturous not because it was a long or difficult drive, but because it was undertaken for the sole purpose of me going to my piano lessons, which I abhorred and rate only slightly better than going to the dentist. I had no real aptitude for playing, didn't care that I had no aptitude for playing, and thought the whole ordeal was a colossal waste of time and money. Suffice it to say we would not be booking Carnegie Hall anytime soon.

After I was released from prison—I mean my lesson—Aniba and I started the drive back to Mosquito. Shortly after we entered ranch property, Ed Lasater, the general manager of the ranches at the time who was at Mosquito for a monthly managers' meeting, drove up from the opposite direction and flagged us down. Ed parked his truck by the side of the road and walked quickly toward our car. I could tell by the look on his face that something serious had happened.

"Don't take Betinha back to the ranch," he told Aniba. "There's been a fire at the house." He saw the panic on my face. "Everyone's all right. No one's been hurt. Don't worry."

I felt a wave of relief, quickly followed by an insatiable curiosity. "Why can't I go back to the house, then?"

"Because the fire's still going, lots of people are working to put it out, but there's nothing for you to do there. You'd just be in the way. Sorry."

I'd just be in the way. That struck a nerve. I wondered where Jimmy, Theresa, and Michael were, and was about to ask, when Ed said to Aniba, "Mr. Emmert says to take her to the Valdelicia's. She can stay the night with them."

That appeased me a tiny bit; I could at least stay with Zenia, my best friend. But I still wanted to go home to see what was happening.

Of course, being a kid in an adult world meant I got no say in the matter. So Aniba dropped me off at Zenia's house in the colony, and as I ran to their front door, I could see smoke rising in the distance. Zenia opened the door and I immediately started to tell her what had happened when her mother stopped me.

"We know," she said, a worried look on her face. Of course they knew: the smoke was pretty self-evident, and most everyone from the colony was already at the house, helping (I was to later learn) quell the fire.

"Come on!" I shouted to Zenia, grabbing her by the arm and heading toward the door.

"No!" Zenia's mother said in a loud voice. "You are to stay here. It is too dangerous."

I begged and pleaded, but Zenia's mom wouldn't budge. "Can we at least go outside and look at the smoke then?" I said rather grumpily.

"Yes. But you two are not to leave the yard."

All I could think at the moment was if I had not been in Presidente Prudente for my stupid piano lesson, I would not have missed the fire.

To say I was ticked off was an understatement. My only solace was that this day marked the end of my piano-playing days. I swore off the instrument, saying I would never again take lessons or play. And I didn't.

The next morning, Zenia and I ate a hurried breakfast of homemade bread, papaya, and coffee with milk, and then we were driven to my house. When we arrived, the pillars in the middle of the house were still smoking. The walls in the kitchen, dining room, and living room didn't exist anymore. They had disintegrated into ember and ash, and the charred pillars stood over them like ghostly sentinels. Bedroom furniture and belongings were strewn all over the yard.

"Oh my gosh," I said, more to myself than to Zenia. I saw Dad coming from the hallway that led to the bedrooms—that part of the house was relatively unscathed. Our house was like a can with the lid peeled back, with the lid in this case being a good chunk of the roof and walls. It was odd to be able to see Dad walking inside the house when I was standing outside. I called out to him and he came over. His face was darkened with soot and his eyes looked puffy and red, probably from lack of sleep. Ranch hands were milling about, and I could hear pounding—it sounded like someone was hammering nails—somewhere down by the horse stables.

"Dad! Where is everyone? Are they okay?"

"Yeah, we're all fine. Our house has seen better days, though." He eyed the dark clouds above and said he had to get the bedroom furniture moved back in before it started to rain.

"You can go talk to your mother," he said. "She can fill you in. She's in the stables right now, I think."

Zenia and I walked down to the stables, where carpenters were indeed working, fashioning them into a makeshift dining room. Other men were converting the tack room, where we kept all the horses' equipment, into a kitchen. Because we *had* no kitchen or dining room anymore. I was in a daze; this didn't seem real. But the acrid, smoky smell in my nose and the ruins of our house told me it was real.

I found Mom with my brothers and sister, and she gave me a fierce hug. When she pulled away from me, her eyes were moist.

"I'm so glad you're okay," she said, her voice breaking. "We're all okay." She looked at my siblings. She half laughed, half cried, and said, "Our *house* isn't okay, but what matters is that we are."

It was an electrical fire, she told me. It started in the wiring above the kitchen ceiling. Jimmy, Theresa, and Michael had been out riding when they saw the smoke in the distance, she said, and galloped home. It was a miracle, really, that half the house was intact, thanks to a bucket brigade—ranch hands, led by Zenia's dad, who used the sprayers normally reserved for spraying the cattle for ticks to hose down the roof and the walls of the bedrooms. They drained the pool in doing so. And people driving by stopped—even a busload of people stopped and lent a hand.

Mom's eyes filled with tears again. "It was a nightmare," she said, "but these people! So many people coming to help, and they didn't even know us! It was just so . . . " She couldn't finish because she was too overwhelmed. She sat down on a bench in the stables.

"Where did you guys sleep last night?" I asked.

"You're looking at it," Jimmy answered solemnly.

"Tonight, though, we can move back into our bedrooms," Mom said.

I couldn't decide if I liked the idea of sleeping in half a house or not. Everything still seemed surreal.

"What about the kitchen and dining room—the *real* rooms, I mean? And the living room? Are we going to rebuild that part of the house?"

"No, we thought we'd try an open-air house," Jimmy deadpanned.

His smart-aleck remark brought me back to my main point of contention yesterday. "Where were you guys when the fire broke out?" I asked.

"We were here. I was riding, and Theresa and Michael were outside the house, playing," Jimmy said. I noticed a slight smug expression on his face: he had seen it; I hadn't. I was pissed, and he knew it.

"Guess you were at your piano lesson, huh," he scoffed.

"I am never playing a piano again for as long as I live!" I shouted, and stomped off, with Zenia following.

Was it silly to be in such a snit about missing the fire? Of course. But remember, I was only nine years old. Mom, on the other hand, had lost some truly valuable and sentimental items, including her prized fine red china, along with many other wedding gifts, not to mention the furnishings and appliances. Material items can be replaced, but sentimental items that are lost are gone forever.

It took many months to rebuild what had been destroyed. But it took only a few hours for my parents to throw a party at what was left of the house. On the same day the fire erupted, once the flames were completely quenched and it was safe to do so, my father gathered the fifty or so ranch hands and volunteers for an announcement.

All of them were exhausted. Many had soot on their faces. Shoulders slumped with fatigue. A few men held the sprayers at their sides that now just dripped water on the ground.

Dad thanked them all in a rather emotional speech (for him), I'm told. The men and women receiving the thanks just nodded and shuffled their feet or looked down at the ground. They didn't want praise. They just wanted to help.

Then my dad shifted gears. A slight grin crept across his face. "I do have one bit of good news," he said, and the heads that had been lowered raised again. "We had cases of beer, gin, and whiskey in our storage room. Those cases are unharmed." He paused a moment, then shouted in glee, "At least we managed to save the booze!" He raised an arm in the air, and cheers went up from the crowd.

"And now," he continued, "we're going to put that booze to good use!"

So, just hours after a fire had destroyed half of our house, with plumes of smoke still rising and darkening the sky, my parents threw a grand party for all the helpers. Spirits revived, toasts were given, and the mood shifted from one of sadness and depression to one of celebration.

Instead of a house half burned down, we had a house still half standing.

You'll remember that my dad was a rodeo guy back in his high school and college days. He loved the atmosphere of a rodeo, the competition, the camaraderie, the cowboys, and, of course, the bulls and horses. It was his way of letting off steam, having a little fun, showing off his skills and athletic abilities (perhaps impressing some of the young ladies in the crowd), and, back then at least, earning some money for college.

When "real life"—in the guise of marriage and kids—came along, his rodeo days largely went by the wayside. But he did occasionally compete even when we were in Brazil, and he rode in a few rodeos, including an annual one in Barretos, about a five-hour drive northeast of Presidente Prudente. This was the *Festa do Peão de Barretos* (Cowboy Festival of Barretos), which was begun in 1955 and has since become world-famous for its size. In our early years in Brazil, Dad made the trip to the festival and competed in bull riding. The announcer made a big deal of him before he rode, saying that he was a famous cowboy "all the way from Texas, USA." During his ride one year, a bull pinned him against a fence, and he suffered some injuries that convinced him it was time to give up competing. He was older than most of the competitors anyway, and he had family and work life to consider.

However, that didn't mean he couldn't still *enjoy* rodeos. So, instead of competing in them, he and Ed Lasater created one for the King Ranches. The rodeos were held at Formosa Ranch, where there were lots of horses and an arena that could be turned into rodeo grounds, complete with a bucking chute, pens, bleachers, and even an announcer's booth—which Dad manned.

All five ranches would send their cowboys and horses to Formosa to compete; we had to leave at 3:00 a.m. on rodeo day to get there in time (dressed, I might add, in brand new western clothes that at least made us look like we belonged at a rodeo). The Geld family—all seven of them—came to watch each year, though they lived several hours away in Tietê. They had no rodeo experience, but they thought it was great fun. People from all over soon flocked to these annual events, and the ranches took it quite seriously: Competitors from each ranch came dressed in their own ranch's colors. They would compete, under the judges' watchful eyes, in various events, including bull riding, steer roping, barrels (where three barrels were placed in a triangular pattern and the rider would ride around each barrel while being timed), and pole bending (where riders would weave a serpentine path around six poles arranged in a line as fast as they could go).

After each rodeo, a huge *churrasco* (barbecue) would be held, with mounds of mouth-watering barbecued beef and various side dishes and desserts available for everyone. These events became massive, and the cowboys had great fun but took the competitions seriously.

So seriously, in fact, that more and more of them were getting banged up as the years went on, injuries that hampered or kept them out of work for a while. Cattle were also getting hurt, as the cowboys would practice nearly year-round. Finally, after ten years, Dad, who was general manager by then, made a rather unpopular decision to shut down the rodeo.

Dad, perhaps hoping that one of his kids would follow in his footsteps, held "kid rodeos" for us kids on Sundays, starting when I was five or six years old. Theresa and I rode barrels, while Jimmy and Michael practiced pole bending. (I kiddingly held claim to being the "second-best barrel racer in my age group in Brazil," because almost no girls my age rode—the only other girl barrel racer in my age group was Rosemary

Lane, the daughter of one of the ranch managers.) I personally could have done without our own version of "Rodeo Days," but Jimmy loved it, and Michael, once he got old enough to ride, was determined to impress his brother and his dad with his riding skills.

And then there's the time that Dad, in his infinite wisdom, had me "compete" against Jimmy in calf riding (no, I was *not* prepping to move up to riding bulls!). I didn't want to, I said I would be no good at it, and I proved it by being thrown off and hitting my head on terra firma, which was *quite* firm at the time. Mom, who happened to be watching, yelled to Dad that I shouldn't be riding, but he walked over to me, picked me up, dusted me off, and held me up as if I were Exhibit A in a court case.

"She's fine!" he hollered back.

If I'd been thinking quicker, I would have faked a concussion. As it was, I merely groused at him, "I am not," but he led me back to my calf and called out to Mom, "Just a few more! Jimmy needs the competition!"

Both Jimmy and Michael were quite athletic, by the way. They both became soccer goalies, and Michael went on to be All-State in Texas in high school, and was goalie for Midwestern State University in Wichita Falls, Texas, which won the national title while he was there.

Those two could follow in Dad's footsteps if they wanted. And Theresa certainly mirrored his love of everything to do with horses and riding. My own footsteps, however, would not be leading me anywhere near a rodeo, unless I was spectating.

I have previously mentioned some of the beliefs of Conceicão, our beloved nursemaid, who was with us from the beginning of our time at Mosquito to the end of our time in Brazil—that is, from 1961 to 1980. Those superstitious beliefs—that if you sweep a broom over someone's feet, that person will never marry; if you wash a mango down with milk, you will die; if you stick a knife into the trunk of a banana tree at midnight, when you pull it out you will hear the name of your future spouse—came from the Afro-Brazilian religion of Candomblé, in which one supreme god reigns, but everyone gets their own personal deity.

The religion held many superstitions about babies and children as well. The afterbirth would be buried in the mother's yard with rue, a bitter, strong-scented herb that was considered a woman's herb. Doing this would keep the family safe from *olho gordo* ("fat eye"), which was jealousy or negative energy toward the baby and the family because of how cute the newborn was. To further prevent *olho gordo*, a mother would tie a red string around her baby's neck until the string essentially rotted off, and older children would wear a red string around their left wrists to also ward off *olho gordo*. If a baby got sick, the mother would go to church and place money at the feet of one of the statues—typically of the Virgin Mary. If older children got sick, their parents would let the kids' hair grow very long. One boy on Mosquito ranch became very sick, and his mother went to the statue of Mary and promised that she would never cut his hair if he got better. (Many people at Mosquito were superstitious; the mother's behavior would not have been seen as strange there.) He did recover, and his mother kept her promise: The boy's hair grew and grew, and he wore it in a long ponytail.

I was intrigued by Candomblé, Conceicão's folklore, and begged her to take me with her to where she worshiped with other believers in Rancharia when we lived at Bartira Ranch; I was twelve or thirteen at the time. She finally acquiesced, and one autumn Saturday evening we drove to Rancharia, parked on a side street in a poor section of town, and walked across the hard-packed dirt that made up the front yard, around the back of this ramshackle house, and into the backyard, where many dark-skinned women in flowing white dresses had gathered. Each woman had her hair tied up, turban-like, with a white scarf. Many men were there also, and they too were dressed in all white—long white shirts hanging over their white pants. Everyone was barefoot, and most of them wore many strings of colored glass beads around their necks.

Moments after we arrived, everyone formed a large circle, and four men began beating rhythmically on the bongos that were held between their knees. The people sang songs in a language I didn't recognize as they swayed to the beat of the drums. Several men were smoking cigars, apparently with the intent of creating a lot of smoke.

Soon, a woman fell into a trance and began swirling in the middle of the circle, her bare feet going round and round on the smooth, hard dirt as the bongos continued their rhythmic beat. Suddenly, the woman let out a shriek and fell to the ground. (Conceicão, a high priestess in Candomblé, later explained that the woman was being possessed by the spirit of Xangô, the god of fire, thunder, and lightning. Xangô historically was revered by the Brazilian slaves because of his strength, resistance, and aggression.) The woman on the ground began convulsing, letting out yelps and groans, shaking and shuddering, as the drums kept beating and the men and women in the circle continued chanting. ("She was next possessed by Iemanjá," Conceicão told me later. "Iemanjá is the goddess of the sea, who watches over sailors and fishermen and controls their catches. She is also the protector of children.") This went on for several minutes; I lost track of time in my fascination for everything that I was seeing and hearing. First one person and then another would go to the center of the circle, swirl around as the drummers continued their pulsating, hypnotic beat as the chanting continued, and then cry out before falling to the ground and convulsing for several minutes. All told, the ceremony lasted probably a couple of hours. During that time, I felt like I was transported to a parallel universe, one where the veil between the living and the dead was paper thin. It felt that way because several times the person in the middle of the circle would receive a message from a dead person's spirit or from some god for someone in the circle. The person receiving the message would be escorted to the middle of the circle to receive it.

I later learned from Conceicão that you could also *ask* to receive a message at the beginning of the ceremony. I returned with her several times to these ceremonies, and once I asked to hear from my maternal grandmother, Hazel, who had died years before. The person in the trance was silent for a bit and then said, "She is well, she sends her blessings to her granddaughter, whom she looks down upon from the skies. She says to take care of your mother, and to give her greetings to her."

Conceicão was many times in the middle of that circle, being possessed by Iemanjá, and receiving and delivering words for people in the circle. "It is exhausting to be in the center," she told me. "It is hard work. But it is important to receive and deliver these messages."

I asked her what it was like to be possessed by one of the gods. "I cannot say," she answered. "You remember nothing when you are in the trance."

Sometimes swords and torches and other items were used during the ceremonies; it was all fascinating to me.

My parents thought the whole thing was very hokey. But I took it seriously. I sometimes took a friend with me, and she would always come back wide-eyed; she knew she had witnessed something serious.

A rather interesting side note: my husband, Jack Schultz, from the American Midwest, bought a farm in Brazil in 1974; I first met Jack in 1980. But a few years before that, Jack had his own experience with Candomblé. In his own words:

"I only had one experience with Candomblé while I was in Brazil, but it was a real eye-opener. One morning, around 2:00 a.m., I was awakened by someone pounding on the door at my house in town. I lived in Dourados, a few miles away, because the farmhouse was rustic, to say the least.

"Anyway, I opened the door to see literally all of my farm workers loaded onto the back of my farm truck. My foreman, Carlos, stepped forward. 'Senhor Schultz, we are sorry, but we are no longer going to stay on the farm.'

"'Carlos, what are you talking about?' I asked, feeling rather bewildered and wondering whatever the issue was, why it couldn't have waited till morning.

"'You have ghosts on your farm! They have been seen with our own eyes. We cannot stay there.'

"I had been in Brazil long enough to know that ghosts were no laughing matter, at least to the people who believed in them. I couldn't afford to lose my laborers. The farmhands slept elsewhere that night, but I convinced Carlos to meet me at the farm the next morning. We met in front of the house, and I noticed Carlos looked nervously around before eyeing me. But there wasn't a cloud in the bright blue sky, or any ghosts floating around, and that calmed his nerves some.

"'All right, Carlos, tell me what you saw,' I said.

"'It wasn't me, Senhor Schultz. It was some of the boys. They told us they saw an old man with a long white beard, and he was walking three feet off the ground.'

"I tried not to roll my eyes. These boys were between eight and twelve years old—prime ages, in my opinion, to 'see' a ghost.

"'Are they sure they saw this man? And that he was walking three feet off the ground?'

"'Yes, yes. They are good boys. They wouldn't lie.'

"I sighed. 'Okay, what do you suggest we do? Because we have to fix this problem.'

"Carlos thought for a moment and then said, 'We bring a priest out here to bless the farm. That should do it.'

"So, we got a priest out to bless the farm and chase the spirits away. The men came back. But it didn't work. People kept seeing the old man with the long white beard, floating above the ground.

"Our next approach was to go to a Candomblé place of worship—in this case, a large front room in a small house in Dourados. Carlos and the other laborers and I took a seat on benches that were placed along the walls. We were instructed by a person—the 'séance assistant,' for lack of better terms—to not untie our shoes or cross our arms or legs. This assistant then drew large white lines in chalk over all of the openings in the room—the windows and doors.

"When this was finished, we waited silently for something to happen. The assistant was silent and had taken a seat along with us. I was beginning to get a bit antsy when suddenly a very large woman—she must have weighed at least 250 pounds—entered the room wearing the traditional long white dress and white head covering that the religion required. This woman, the high priestess, was smoking a very long and very thick cigar. She walked slowly in front of each of us seated on the benches, stopping to blow smoke directly in our faces. Then she began to speak in some sort of tongue; it sounded almost like pig Latin, but in Portuguese, with likely some African words mixed in.

"Then she moved to the center of the room, closed her eyes, and listened. For what? A message from the dead, I guess. From the spirit of the old man who was haunting my farm.

"But she opened her eyes, said nothing, and exited the room. I looked questioningly at her assistant.

"'Go,' she said. 'Come back next week.'

"We came back four times over the next month. Same benches, same chalk lines, same big woman, same (or similar) big cigar. Same smoke and pig Latin. And same silence at the end, for the first three return visits. I could only be thankful that my laborers had found places to lodge in town.

"On our fourth visit back, however, the high priestess with the large stogey announced at the end of the ceremony, 'I know why your farm is haunted.'

"Everyone on the benches stirred, me included. We were all ears.

"'The former owner of the farm had not been properly paid for the property and has come back to haunt it,' the high priestess said.

"I immediately thought, 'Well, hell, I paid for the farm once already. Am I going to have to pay for it again to chase the spook away?'

"I posed this question to the high priestess. To my relief, she replied, 'Go and get a bottle of cachaça, a bottle of red wine, some white candles, a plate of un-popped popcorn, and a dead chicken, and bring it to your farmhouse.'

"That, I could do. So I gathered the items, brought them out to the farm, and the large, cigar-smoking priestess held a séance out there. We then marched into the woods near the farm and left the offering there. If the ghost of the former owner didn't drink the wine and cachaça (a distilled spirit made from fermented sugarcane juice), someone did, because I checked a couple of weeks later, and everything was gone. I wondered if he had a popcorn popper wherever he stayed.

"I didn't care who or what drank the spirits. What I cared about was having hired laborers who weren't afraid to work on the farm and who weren't looking over their shoulders for ghosts of old bearded dead men.

"Say what you will: We never had problems with any ghosts on that farm again."

On another unusual side note, my interest was piqued when I heard of Ana Maria, a fortuneteller in Martinopolis, a neighboring town about thirty miles away. I was twelve years old when I first started going to her, and I went to her for many years. (I could have chosen to go to a priest from the Umbanda folk religion, which combined elements of macumba, Roman Catholicism, and South American Indian practices, but I was enthralled by the idea of a fortuneteller using cards to tell my future.) Again, my parents thought this was hokey, but they allowed me to go. "They're just going to tell you what you want to hear," my dad said. Ana Maria was pretty intimidating; she was huge, with jet-black hair and large, rather scary-looking eyes. In the room she told fortunes in, pictures of macumba gods hung on the walls, with a different-colored candle hanging under each picture. She always burned incense when I was there; my eyes would water when I visited her.

One time, toward the end of my visits with her, she told me that the boy I had been dating—whose name began with a "J" and who had dark hair (this was correct)—was not who I would end up with. I would end up with someone who was not as tall, but who also had dark hair and whose name began with a "J."

My dad, of course, scoffed at this. My boyfriend at the time, Jimmy Herbert, was six feet, six inches tall, and "dark hair" was a pretty easy prediction.

Well, all I can say is this: I ended up marrying a dark-haired man who, at six feet tall, was indeed shorter than my old boyfriend. My husband's name? Jack.

I had the last laugh on Dad with that one.

When I was ten and we were living at Mosquito Ranch, I developed seed warts on my knees, a virus that spread to my lower legs. They spread because I would accidentally scratch the warts on the side of the pool, causing them to bleed—and which also caused everyone else to nervously scold me, because the virus was very contagious. I went to a doctor and had liquid nitrogen applied to freeze the warts off, but that was only minimally helpful, and even though some were frozen off, new ones would appear. One of our maids suggested rubbing the warts with corn and then feeding the corn to a black virgin chicken. My warts remained, but the chicken seemed quite happy. (Conceicão told me it probably didn't work because the chicken was really a rooster, or the hen was not really a virgin.)

Another maid suggested I go to a *curandeiro* (faith healer). This *curandeiro* was an old woman who lived in a thatched-roof hut in a rustic settlement of huts within a mile of our house. The people who lived in this little settlement were charged with clearing the milkweed trees from the ranch's pastures—a constant, nearly year-round battle.

Desperate to get rid of the warts, I went to see the *curandeiro* one early evening around dusk. She invited me inside her little two-room hut, which was dark even though it was bright outside. The hut had no electricity; a kerosene lantern sat on a table in the middle of the main room. Several family members were in the hut with her, but she kicked them out so we could be alone. The woman appeared to be ancient; her face was a mass of wrinkles, and her dark eyes were so deep-set in her face that they were hard to see. When she smiled, I noticed that most of her teeth were missing. We talked a bit, and then she said, "Child, you came at exactly the right time. Tomorrow night. There will be a full moon then."

"It has to be a full moon?"

"Why of course it does. Don't you know that?"

I allowed that I didn't.

"Tomorrow night, bring me a can of peaches, a long white candle, and some black tobacco. You hear? And come back when the moon is good and high in the sky, along about nine o'clock. Not before."

The idea of meeting this *curandeiro* at night was more than a little freaky to me; I was equal parts curious, excited, and scared the next night as I ran to her place, a flashlight illuminating my path. Out of breath, I showed up at her hut around nine with the items she had mentioned. She welcomed me in her hut, which had a dirt floor and just a few pieces of furniture, took the tobacco I brought, rolled it in thick brown paper, and began smoking it. It both looked and smelled more like a cigar than a cigarette. Soon, her little hut was filled with the smoke, which smelled rich and strong.

She took the candle and set it on her table, near the kerosene lantern that gave off a soft, dim glow. She already had a few other candles burning to augment the kerosene lamp's light. She then took the can of peaches and held it in her hand. I looked at the can, wondering how it was going to come into play. She saw me peering at the can.

"You are wondering what I'm going to do with the peaches?"

I nodded, waiting in anticipation. How could peaches heal warts?

"Why, child, I'm going to do what anyone does with a can of peaches." She set the can on a little shelf behind her, with other cans of food, then turned back to me. "When I get hungry for peaches, I'll eat 'em." She gave me another near-toothless grin. "And I'm *always* hungry for peaches."

So, the peaches, the tobacco, and the candle were really payment for her services, I guessed. She grabbed a metal bowl, walked past me, went outside, and came back in a few moments later. The bowl now had water and some small leaves in it. She also had a couple of plant branches in her hand. She set the branches and the bowl on the table.

"What's—"

She held her hand up, quieting me. Her eyes closed, and she began chanting in some ancient tongue, doubtless an African language. She chanted for a minute or two, her eyes closed the entire time, and the rhythm of her chant reminded me of the Candomblé ceremonies I had attended with Conceicão.

The chanting came to an abrupt stop and she opened her eyes and looked at me. "All right now, pick up the bowl of water. Quickly, child!"

I hurried to the table to pick up the bowl.

"Now go to the door and toss the water out, without turning your body around. You face me and toss it over your shoulder. Go! Go!"

I did as she instructed, feeling both a bit foolish and a bit scared. "Now what?"

"Now you go home and wait. I'm going to hang those branches upside down, and once they're dried, your warts will be gone." She explained it was the leaves from those branches that were in the water.

"How long will it take?" I asked.

"About a month, child. Before the next full moon, your warts will be gone. Every one of them."

A doctor had tried to freeze them off. That didn't work. The maid's approach of rubbing corn on my warts and then feeding the corn to a black chicken didn't pan out. But something about this experience—perhaps the utter surety of the old woman—had me believing that this remedy would actually do the trick. Even though she had never touched the warts, and no medicine had directly touched them.

I offered to pay her money, but she said that's what the candle, peaches, and tobacco were for. If she took money for her services, her faith-healing powers would leave her.

"Well, thank you," I said as I moved to her door. She merely nodded and turned away as I walked out. As I ran home, still spooked, I imagined her opening that can of peaches and enjoying the sweet treat.

My family all kidded me about my visit to the faith healer. "Your warts will just leave on their own," my dad said. "You're lucky that old witch didn't make your legs fall off!" Jimmy said. "You better hope she didn't put a curse on you!" Michael chimed in.

But the maids believed. And so did I.

By the time the next full moon rolled around, the warts had vanished.

CHAPTER 10

MEANWHILE, 7,000 MILES NORTH . . .

"HEY, LOOK AT WHAT I GOT!" Jimmy said, running up to us—our whole family plus Grandpa Green, Mom's dad—in the William P. Hobby Airport in Houston, Texas. My ten-year-old brother proudly held up a three-pack of rubbers, which he got when he dropped a quarter into a vending machine in a men's lavatory.

"Jimmy, those are *not* for you!" Mom said, snatching the rubbers out of his hand.

"But, Mom! I bought them with my own money!"

"What are they?" Theresa said, trying to get a look at what Mom held in her hands. Mom covered the packaging so no one could see it.

"None of your business. Or *his*," Mom added, nodding to a forlorn Jimmy.

"Good Lord," Grandpa Green muttered, shaking his head, while Dad tried to conceal a smirk.

"It wasn't even your money!" I hissed at Jimmy. I enjoyed jumping on the bandwagon when one of my siblings—especially Jimmy—was in hot water with Mom or Dad.

"Was so! Grandpa gave it to me!"

Which was true. I suppose, in a court of law, the transference had taken place, and the coins were his. But that didn't stop me from rubbing it in.

And thus began one of our trips back to Texas, generally taken annually, in the spring. One of the first things Grandpa Green did when we arrived was to give each of us kids a huge handful of coins. We were his only grandkids, and he loved doting on us—even if he did think we were kind of wild at times. We didn't have vending machines in Brazil, at least where we were, so to drop coins in a machine and get something in return was a big thrill for us. It didn't really matter much what it was—gum, candy, soda, trinkets, toys, or, heaven forbid, rubbers—it was just the *idea* of it. In Texas, we were in a brave new world, one that was very different from Brazil.

We'd usually visit for about a month, spending time with Grandpa Green and also with Buck (he refused to be called "Grandpa" or anything other than "Buck") and Grandma Emmert. The time between our visits back to Texas seemed like forever, and memories of Texas and our relatives there seemed to blur when we were in Brazil, but once we returned to the Lone Star State, those memories came flooding back as if we had been away just a month or so.

Pretty much *everything* was a thrill during those trips—the coins and vending machines; Grandpa's car, a huge Mercury Grand Marquis, bigger than any car we'd ever seen; the cars my dad would rent, which were different and somehow seemed more exotic than the cars back in Brazil; the escalators we'd go up and down on in the department stores; the television shows—oh, the television shows! Remember, back in Brazil, we had a black-and-white TV that had one channel that aired shows created for adults—soaps and serials that kids normally wouldn't be interested in. But in America, they had *cartoons!* We sat, fascinated, in front of Grandpa's TV in the mornings, watching *Tom & Jerry, Bugs Bunny, The Flintstones, Underdog,* and many more. And on color TV! We also tuned into *The Beverly Hillbillies, I Dream of Jeannie,* and other shows with real actors who weren't dubbed—unlike the shows in Brazil.

Perhaps because of Jimmy's purchase of rubbers, or more likely just because of our general exuberance and unfettered joy at being in the US, where things were so marvelously different than in Brazil, Grandpa half-jokingly called us "little savages" and told my mom that she should enroll us in school. (We typically arrived in Texas when there were still a few months left in the school year.) No doubt Grandpa, while he both loved and spoiled us, wanted a balance of joyous bedlam and peace in his house during our stay.

Perhaps my mother wanted the same, because one year she promptly enrolled us in school in Rockport, about a half hour from Sinton, where Grandpa lived and where Mom grew up. We were renting a house in Rockport at the time. (Our vacations in the States were always split between Grandpa's house, Buck's ranch, and rentals—at various places in South Texas, usually along the coast.)

"It'll be fun," Mom said. "See what it's like in an American school. Plus, you can make friends there and have something to do."

Translated, of course, that meant *You can stay out of trouble and out of Grandpa's hair.* And I suspect there was a bit of curiosity in her, wanting to know how her children would fare in an American school. Would they be at the top of the class?

We didn't mind; it was part of the adventure, and she was right: It *would* be fun to see what school was like in the US. And, in Jimmy's ever-scheming mind, it would also be fun to lead on the US kids.

For example, one year, when Jimmy was ten years old, the teacher in the classroom that he was visiting asked him to come to the front of the class, talk a bit about how it was to live in Brazil, and answer questions the students had.

Ever the showman, Jimmy strolled to the front of the class, leaned against the teacher's desk, and began telling tall tales.

"Well, a lot of people don't know this, but I was born in a tree house," Jimmy started, and the kids' eyes grew large.

"Whoa."

"You lived in a tree house?"

"Yeah, our first few years we lived in a tree house that my dad built. It was in the middle of a jungle near a river that had piranha in it. One of the little kids who lived nearby fell into the river once, and when she came out she was screaming and had only a bloody stump where her left hand was."

A couple of girls screamed, covering their mouths, while a few boys said, "Cool!"

Another boy asked, "Why'd you have to live in a tree house? Don't they have real houses in Brazil?"

"Yeah, but they were building a house for us on our ranch, which had this jungle on the edge of it. One morning I woke up and felt this python tightening around my cot and my waist. I was being suffocated by it! I could barely breathe. But Dad got up and hacked it to pieces with a machete. He saved my life."

"Whoa!" several kids said. Jimmy glanced over at the teacher, who arched an eyebrow while looking just a tad doubtful. He knew he had to reel it in, but he couldn't resist one more humongous stretch of the truth.

"You had to watch where you were stepping in the jungle," he said. "One time, when I wasn't careful, I was bit by a poisonous snake. My leg swelled up to like twice its size. My dad had to make a cut in my leg where the fangs had gone in and then suck out a bunch of blood and venom and spit it out. So, he really saved my life twice."

One girl looked like she was about to faint. Several others said, "Eww!" and one looked like she was going to throw up.

"Jimmy," the teacher said. He gave her an innocent look.

"Yes ma'am?"

"Maybe we should stop there."

"But don't you want to hear about the voodoo healers? We had a bunch of—"

"No, I think that's enough for now," the teacher said. "Why don't you take your seat and we'll move on to our geography lesson."

You can bet on the playground at noon that Jimmy was like a rock star, surrounded by a horde of boys who wanted more gruesome details of the purported life he lived in Brazil.

However, he was not quite the rock star when Mom got wind of his tall tales.

"You made us sound like heathens!" she said. "Like worse than those stupid Beverly Hillbillies! Living in trees, being bitten by snakes? And they believed all that malarkey?"

"I just thought it would be funny—" Jimmy started.

"Funny! Making your family out to be living like savages? We'll be the laughingstock of town! Why didn't you tell them about our beautiful house, all the maids and cooks and drivers we have, how important your Dad is, how many cattle we have, what we're doing down there in the first place for Swift?"

Jimmy shrugged, looking properly chastised. "I don't know. That stuff's just sort of . . . boring."

Mom just shook her head and rolled her eyes and walked away, muttering to herself as she did.

We loved staying with Grandpa in Sinton and also living in our rentals for a few weeks near the beach. Our trips to Buck's were not as much fun, mainly because there were no kids our age there to play with. Also, it was a ranch—and we were experiencing plenty of ranch living already in Brazil. And Buck, while I know he loved us, didn't know how to show it. When he was around us, he'd stare at us for a moment, trying to think of something to say, and then he'd talk about people we didn't know, or about cutting hay or doing some sort of pasture maintenance . . . all stuff that was lovely material for insomniacs, but didn't exactly thrill young kids.

Grandma, on the other hand, knew how to relate to us kids—especially me. She taught me how to use a sewing machine during our trips back to Texas, how to use paper patterns, which I would later do back in Brazil. She'd dote on me in many ways. She let me stay in my Aunt

North Padre Island, home leave 1970. Author collection.

Ann's room while Aunt Ann was away at college. I loved Aunt Ann's doll collection, and Grandma, knowing my love for dolls, gave me the room but told me not to touch the dolls, but to just look at them. I, of course, promptly started playing with them once I was alone, and in short order I managed to lose one of the doll's shoes. You'd think a doll shoe wouldn't be that hard to find, but, at least in this instance, you'd be wrong. Getting more and more desperate, having searched exceedingly well in all the places the shoe *wasn't*, I finally went to Grandma and confessed that I *might* have been playing with one of the dolls and it was *possible* that one of the shoes was missing. Expecting a mild tongue lashing (Grandma was too sweet to ever get very mad), instead I got a sympathetic smile and a pat on the head as she said, "Let's go look for it, dear."

But the shoe was apparently a magic shoe that could disappear off the face of the earth, or at least from Aunt Ann's room; we never did find it.

"Well, Aunt Ann probably won't even notice it," Grandma said after we gave up the search.

"I'm sorry."

"It's okay, dear."

"I won't play with them anymore. I promise."

"No, go ahead. I know it's too great a temptation for you to be in here and not play with them. Just don't tell your Aunt Ann." She winked at me and left me alone in the room.

Grandma's sweetness balanced out Buck's gruffness. The love and care that he had inside but couldn't show just seemed to pour naturally out of her.

Every time we stayed with Buck and Grandma, Grandma would get excited and say she wanted to come visit us in Brazil. One time we were all sitting around the kitchen table, talking about such a trip.

"You're always welcome," Dad said. "You and Buck both."

"Yes! Please come! It would be so much fun!" we kids chimed in. "We can show you around, you can meet our friends, we can go into town, even to São Paulo. It'll be a blast!"

"When are we going to have time to come down to Brazil?" Buck growled. "It's not like I've got a lot of time on my hands to traipse half-way around the world."

"It's not halfway around the world," Mom said. "It's not such a bad trip, and you could see parts of the world you've never seen."

"Yes, just imagine that, Buck!" Grandma said, her eyes glowing with hope. "Wouldn't it be fun to travel a bit, see where they live, see what it's like in another country?" Poor Grandma. She rarely if ever got to travel. This would be the trip of a lifetime for her.

"I know where they live," Buck said. "Brazil. We see them when they come back here, anyway."

"Well, if you're too busy, maybe Mom could just come on her own," my dad said.

Buck gave Dad a look like *That'll never happen.*

"Or if money's a concern, we can pay for her travel," Dad added.

"Did I say money was an issue?" Buck snarled.

"No, but—"

"I've got work to do." And with that, Buck got up, grabbed his work hat, and headed outside.

Grandma never made it down to Brazil. Neither, of course, did Buck. I thought it was grossly unfair of Buck not to at least let Grandma come down—especially if we were going to pay her way—but Buck was never one to care much what others thought about his decisions.

One Sunday while staying with Buck and Grandma, we went with them to their Catholic church. Buck was horrified when we didn't know the liturgical responses or the prayers that were uttered aloud by everyone in the congregation.

"Do you not go to Mass down there?" he muttered to Dad as we walked out of church.

"Well, Sundays kind of get away from us."

"Hell, Latin America has about a billion Catholics. You ought to be able to find a church down there somewhere."

My dad didn't care that much, but Mom was always one for decorum, so for once she sided with Buck, and it was decided that, as I was eight years old, it was high time that I had my First Communion. The ceremony signifies that a person has received the sacrament of the eucharist, the body and blood of Jesus.

That next Saturday, decked out in a traditional white stiff toile first communion dress complete with white veil, I went to the church to practice the ceremony. I absolutely loved that dress and imagined it as my "princess dress." I was excited to receive first communion—but I was *not* happy when I learned that the kids were to walk down the aisle toward the altar in pairs. I wanted the spotlight on me! I didn't want to share it with someone else (who would be blocking some views of my pretty dress, by the way), and particularly not with the redheaded boy they stuck me with.

I complained to the nun who was in charge of the practice that I was *not* going to walk down the aisle with that kid or with anyone else, but she firmly told me that indeed I was, if I wanted to receive first communion. So I sulked, and stewed, and fumed, and plotted, and the next day, walking down the aisle with this freckle-faced redheaded kid, I gave the boy a shove and he tripped and fell and started bawling. I kept on walking, my eyes front and center, a picture of pure innocence as I approached the altar.

After the ceremony, the lady in charge walked briskly up to me, the little redheaded kid in tow. His face was tear-streaked and he was still sniffling.

"Betinha, what got into you that you had to push Paul down?"

"I didn't push him. He just tripped over his own feet."

"I did not! You pushed me!"

"Betinha, I want you to apologize to Paul. I and many others saw you push him. There's no use denying it."

"Well, even if I did push him, if he weren't so clumsy, he wouldn't have fallen. You can't blame me just because he's clumsy."

"Betinha. I want you to apologize. Now."

"No!"

Just as the lady was about to reprimand me, Mom walked up and dug her fingers into my arm. "So sorry, we need to go!" she said to the lady. "We're late for a celebration at home!" Before the lady could say anything, Mom whisked me away. I thought I might be in worse trouble with her, but she wasn't upset at all. She just kept saying how beautiful I looked in that white dress.

Unfortunately, that white dress did not last another twenty-four hours. The next day, I walked into Grandma's laundry room to see Mom taking my white dress, now dyed pink, out of the washer.

"It's so you can wear it again!" Mom said when I began to cry.

"But it's supposed to be *white*!" I said. "It was my princess dress!"

"Oh. But it's pretty in pink, too, don't you think?"

My wailing answered that question. I ran into my bedroom, slammed the door, and threw myself on the bed. I cried some more, thought how cruel the world was, and recalled how beautiful I was in that pristine white dress just the day before. The image of me shoving that little redheaded kid over flashed in my mind.

Doubtless that little boy would be laughing hard if he saw me now.

One year—when I was six, in 1964—our trip back to Sinton was immortalized in the county newspaper. A near full-page article, accompanied by a photo of our family and titled "Brazil is Home to Pete Emmert Family," made us famous (at least in my mind). It talked about how our ranch—we were at Mosquito at the time—was being used to introduce Santa Gertrudis cattle to Brazil and how our ranch had thirty-six thousand acres with twenty thousand head of cattle and seventy-five employees (statistics Mom no doubt wished Jimmy had shared with his Texan classmates, rather than the horror stories he made up). It mentioned Jimmy and me by name—my name was in print!—saying how we learned to speak Portuguese before English.

Mom was quoted in the article as saying, "It is a completely different kind of life, and when you first arrive everything is completely unusual, but it grows on you. For men it is more interesting and offers more of a challenge. Brazil has lots of good opportunities, but you have to decide if you will stay for the long term."

We were obviously in it for the long haul, as evidenced by Jimmy's response when asked if he wanted to remain in the US. "No, I want to go back home."

Home to us was Brazil.

Brazil, the land that is home to almost 60 percent of the Amazon rainforest and to more species of monkeys than anywhere else in the world. The land with the world's longest beach, at more than twenty-four thousand feet, and the world's biggest carnival, the Rio Carnival, which began nearly three hundred years ago and attracts more than 2 million people per day for its six-day annual festivals. The land that is longer than any country in the world, at about 2,800 miles, and that is home to Iguazú Falls, which is situated on the Brazilian-Argentine border and is the world's largest waterfall.

And the land where we kids were raised, on five Swift-King Ranches, amidst thousands and thousands of cattle and horses and hundreds of friends, ranch hands, and townsfolk of varying races, colors, creeds, and ethnicities.

Our return trips to Brazil were always bittersweet. We loved our month-long visits to the US to see family, stay on the coast, and enjoy the amenities that we didn't have in Brazil (the vending machines, the TV shows, the fancy cars we would rent). Having grown up in Brazil, that country truly was our home, and it's always good to return home, but we did so with sighs and forlorn feelings in our hearts. Sort of like

Emmert Family on Delta Steamship Lines. Author collection.

Dorothy leaving Oz to head back to Kansas—she couldn't wait to get back to her home and family, but she was heartbroken at leaving the amazing land she had discovered and all the new friends she had made.

We would usually return to Brazil by ship, because we typically couldn't fit everything we brought back on a plane. I'm not just talking a few souvenirs; I'm talking large tanks of bull semen for our Santa Gertrudis cattle (certainly not your typical souvenir there!), tree horns for making saddles, maybe some saddles themselves. Not to mention ropes, bits, bridles, and more saddle-making gear. Rather difficult to stash all that in the overhead bins.

So, we would board a Delta Line ship out of the Houston port. (On a few occasions we left from New Orleans—including 1961, when I was just three and the year Hurricane Carla hit. Carla is ranked as the most intense US tropical cyclone ever, and we had to leave a few days early to make it safely out of port.) The shipping line had built three state-of-the-art ships, with unique designs to cater to passenger/cargo services to South America. Built back in the 1940s, these ships were constructed at a cost of $7 million each, an impressive outlay at the time. They were the first commercial ships in the world to be equipped with "post-war radar," giving officers a clear view at three ranges: two, six, and thirty nautical miles.

It was a real treat for us to board these massive ocean liners and float through the Gulf of Mexico, the Caribbean Sea, and the Atlantic Ocean as we made our leisurely way back to the Santos port—a distance of almost 4,500 nautical miles (and over 5,100 miles in non-nautical terms). We made stops at the island of Curaçao; La Guaira, a capital city in Venezuela; Rio de Janeiro; and, finally, Santos. The trip back would take twelve days.

It was like ending our trip with a luxury cruise. We had air-conditioning, swimming pools, fine dining, entertainment, activities and games, and costume parties—Jimmy and I were dressed as Indians one year, with my mom, pregnant with Theresa at the time, dressed as an Indian woman. There were lots of decks to lounge on. The ship always threw a big costume party when we crossed the equator. So, while we were sad to be leaving the US, it's not like we didn't enjoy our return trip.

Except for the year a group of older boys (from missionary families) told me, when I was six years old, that they were going to throw me overboard if they caught me alone on the deck. To be honest, I never enjoyed leaning over the rails of the upper decks, anyway. I'd get a bit dizzy and fear I was going to fall overboard on my own. I made sure to stick close to my parents the year those boys threatened to toss me overboard. Obviously, they were just trying to scare me—and it worked! I developed a dislike for missionaries after this.

Once we docked at Santos, a company driver would pick us up and take us to São Paulo, where we would catch a train back to the closest town near the ranch. By this time, we were tired and just ready to be home; the excitement and allure of being on a huge ocean liner was over, and we were back in familiar territory. So, the last leg of the journey always seemed to last forever, and our crankiness level got turned up a notch or two. But once we got home, we kids were the envy of our friends, because we had all these cool new American toys and clothes, and we seamlessly moved back into our old life, the life we had always known, our Brazilian life.

We missed America, we missed our relatives, we missed the excitement of the trip and the newness of nearly everything we came across in the US—but we were back home again, where we belonged.

Jimmy Emmert and Betinha, Fazenda Mosquito. Author collection.

CHAPTER 11

OF STARSKY & HUTCH AND OTHER VISITORS

WHEN YOU LIVE ON A RANCH IN THE MIDDLE OF NOWHERE—which might as well have been our address for all three ranches we lived on—you look for any sort of excitement you can find to spice up your otherwise boring and monotonous days. (Remember, this is from a kid's perspective: Life on a ranch was far from dull for the cowboys and other ranch hands who kept the ranch running through their blood, sweat, and occasional curses.) The boredom we kids experienced on the ranch led to the pranks we played on our guests, the shenanigans we pulled, and the stunts we (thankfully) lived through. My siblings and I had different interests, but when guests arrived, we united and focused on our common enemy for the duration of their stay. We had to stir up some fun, or we'd go crazy.

So, you can imagine how excited we were when we had visitors to our ranch—which was relatively often. And we had an array of them: those sent by King Ranch executives to see firsthand how a ranch could be effectively operated in the tropics; King Ranch relatives who lived all over the world; Brazilian ranchers and farmers who were interested in buying some of the ranch's unique Santa Gertrudis cattle or quarter horses; horse trainers from Texas who would put on roping and cutting clinics (these trainers became part of the foundation of the Brazilian Quarter Horse Association); and many others.

As kids, our main duties were to line up and greet the guests, pretend to be well behaved, and hang around until we were dismissed.

If our guests had kids our age, we would be in charge of entertaining them—which proved to be interesting on occasion. Sometimes we would get city folk with rather snobby children who thought they knew everything; they soon learned they didn't know *quite* everything—such as how to ride a horse for two hours straight while still being able to sit in a dinner chair a bit later on. Or, more simply, how to ride a horse, period. Many times rather snotty children would be tossed from their horses, and we would conceal our smirks long enough to encourage them to get right back on, they were getting the hang of it, and the horse would buck them off again, or they would just fall off on their own because they had no clue how to stay on a horse. This provided us with great entertainment on otherwise dull and hot afternoons.

With the kids we liked a bit more, we would sometimes sneak down to the colony after dinner, in the dark, and involve them firsthand in a few pranks: twisting the TV antennas on a few houses and running off before anyone could come outside and catch us; throwing stones on the metal roof of the machine shop and having the stones clatter as they rolled down the roof; and engaging in "stone wars" with a family of fifteen that we shared a mutual distaste with. We would throw stones and rocks at each other, hiding behind fences and trees. Once, one of our friends was hit by a stone pretty hard, leaving a big bruise, and this jolted a bit of sense into both sides as we realized the danger and stupidity of throwing projectiles that could put someone's eye out. So we backed off the stone wars.

We would also ride horses through the colony at breakneck speed, scattering dogs and children and chickens in our path (more than a few chickens met their early demise this way). As I think back, I realize we could have seriously injured a child—at times mothers had to yank toddlers up from the road just before we passed through, screaming like banshees—and I am eternally grateful that nothing bad happened during such misadventures. I am also thankful for the kindness and tolerance of the adults in the colonies—had they told our parents what we were doing, we'd have been spanked with a belt and forced to endure the wrath of our mother. I'm not sure which would have been harder.

Bob Kleberg Jr., the grandson of King Ranch founder Richard King and the president of King Ranch, Inc., when Dad was managing the ranches, was a frequent visitor to Brazil. "Mr. Bob," as he was universally known, would check in on all five ranches, but spend most of his time on the two ranches that King owned solely (Mosquito and Formosa; Swift owned Bartira and Laranja Doce, and the two corporations jointly owned Brasilandia. The profits from all five ranches were split fifty-fifty between the two corporations).

Mr. Bob ran the King Ranches from 1932 until he died in 1974. He was third in the line of those who ran the ranches, starting with Richard King, who founded King Ranch in 1853 with Gideon Lewis. King died in 1885 and was followed by Bob Kleberg Sr., who served as Richard King's, and King Ranch's, legal counsel (though King's widow, Henrietta, was a dominant force in the running of the ranch as well, until her death in 1925). When the elder Kleberg passed away in 1932, Bob Kleberg Jr. took over ranch operations.

By the time I met Bob Kleberg Jr., he was in his early seventies, but he was still fit and handsome, and he looked every inch the cowboy and rancher that he was. (In fact, though it was estimated he was worth more than $100 million when he died in 1974 at age seventy-eight, he said in an interview that he always considered himself a rancher.) As a younger man, Mr. Bob had movie star looks—and if Hollywood needed a horseman, they needed to look no further than Mr. Bob, who never went anywhere without his tan Stetson.

Mr. Bob was the driving force behind the expansion of King Ranch into South America, Australia, and other locations across the globe. In fact, when he died, King Ranch owned 960,000 acres of cattle and oil lands in Texas—and 11.5 million acres of ranch land abroad. It was Mr.

Bob who crossed Indian Brahmin bulls with English shorthorn cattle to produce Santa Gertrudis; the Indian Brahmins could weather the heat well, and that's why the Santa Gertrudis, officially recognized as a new breed in 1940 by the US Department of Agriculture, flourished so well in tropical climes.

Mr. Bob also bred quarter horses, which are tremendous work horses and profited the ranches greatly, and he loved thoroughbreds. Two of his horses, Assault and Middleground, were Kentucky Derby winners; in fact, Assault won the coveted Triple Crown in 1946 by sweeping the Derby, the Preakness, and the Belmont Stakes.

All of this is pretty heady stuff. But you would never know it by being around Mr. Bob. He was a down-to-earth, unpretentious guy who dressed to work—that is, in khakis and work shirts and his ever-present Stetson—and who loved nothing better than to ride with the cowboys on the ranch, join in with them on whatever the tasks of the day were, and share a meal at the chuck wagon with them. He did this often while he visited the ranches, and he treated the ranch hands and everyone else the same as he would a visiting luminary: with respect and dignity. He would shake each cowboy's hand, ask him about his family, and converse with him as if they had known each other for a while. This would catch many of the cowboys by surprise; they came to look forward to his visits, to the big boss who worked alongside of them and treated them as equals.

Mr. Bob's unpretentiousness was hardly an act. I later learned that back in Texas, this man who was worth many tens of millions of dollars, lived in a seven-room house and operated out of a small, cluttered office in Kingsville. Near his humble abode was a twenty-five-room mansion, reserved primarily for guests to King Ranch. Mr. Bob was much more interested in working, in expanding the ranching business, in devoting his time to his other businesses—a bank, a newspaper, a lumberyard, and others—and in developing forest-felling equipment and land-clearing devices to turn unworkable tracts of land into lush pastures, than he was in sitting back and luxuriating in all the wealth he and his family had accumulated. Money simply gave him the means to do more of the things he loved. And what he loved most was ranching.

When Mr. Bob came to Brazil, he would stay with us for about a week, usually accompanied by his assistant, John Cypher, who worked on King Ranch for over forty years and who wrote a book about Mr. Bob and King Ranch. Mr. Bob's sister, Mary Etta Kleberg, who went by "Etta" (we jokingly called her "Dry Etta," because she didn't drink), would also often come on these visits, and they would bring us presents. One year, Etta brought me a beautiful, sparkling opal kangaroo brooch from Australia. They were kind and generous people.

Mr. Bob and Dad and other ranch managers would meet at the guest house at Bartira, talking all things ranching, but what Mr. Bob and Dad did most on these visits was get out, explore the ranches, check out the Santa Gertrudis and the quarter horses, inspect the pastures and fences, and, as I mentioned, ride and work with the cowboys. They would also reserve a bit of time for some quail hunting, and a houseboy would accompany them in their vehicle, ready to serve them a Bourbon Old Fashioned to quench their thirst. The week before Mr. Bob and his small entourage would come down, the ranch was buzzing with excitement and preparation. The week he was there was a huge highlight for the ranch. And the week after he left was always a bit of a letdown, sort of like Christmas passing, with life going back to normal.

We had plenty of other visitors, too, including a number of dignitaries. A Spanish princess and her boyfriend visited the ranch, and I was thrilled when she asked if I could go riding with her and her boyfriend (along with a cowboy who got the horses ready and accompanied us). She was very beautiful, dressed to the nines in her English riding clothes and Spanish leather boots, and I was impressed that she rode with an English saddle. Her boyfriend laced his fingers together, creating a place for her to step so he could gently lift her up into the saddle. The next day, I told Jimmy this, and demanded that he help me up into my saddle, and he promptly helped me up—but instead of gently lifting me, he gave me a shove that sent me tumbling over the horse and falling to the ground on the other side. So much for wanting to be treated like royalty.

The vice president of Brazil came out with the American ambassador; we were not very impressed with the vice president. Brazil was in a military dictatorship at the time, and this man was a military type, not very educated or sophisticated, filling a hollow title. Still, Brazil's secret service came out before the visit and demanded that lots of bushes be cut so they could see through them to protect the VP and the ambassador. We thought this was silly, and could have done without the visit, but we didn't have a choice. So, our bushes got a haircut.

The highlight of this visit happened as we had our dinner outside. We could easily see the security detail lurking around the trimmed bushes—and our dogs could both see and smell them, and gave chase to the secret service men, who took off running as Mom was frantically calling the dogs off. We kids, of course, loved the unexpected entertainment—though a quick warning glance from Mom told us we'd better keep our merriment to ourselves.

Daniel Ludwig, who was number one on the first Forbes 400 Richest Americans list in 1982, came out to the ranch in the early '70s. He had bought 1.6 million acres of land in the Amazonian Basin, on the north bank of the river, and planned to build a tropical tree farm for a pulp paper factory that he constructed on the land. He cleared land to plant two varieties of trees to be harvested for his factory, built a twenty-six-mile railroad and three thousand miles of trails and roads, and raised cattle and planted fifteen thousand acres of rice to feed the thirty thousand workers who lived in his settlements. He visited the ranch to consult with Dad about how to develop the land for what became known as his "Jari project" (named for the location on the lower reaches of the Rio Jari, a tributary of the Amazon River).

Ludwig was a rather humorless and dour man; I'm not sure I ever saw him smile. He was also, we learned, very particular about his bananas.

During his visit, he requested a certain type of banana. Note that Brazil has about ten varieties of bananas—even though the fruit is not native to the country, being brought there by the Portuguese. The fruit has certainly flourished in Brazil, as it is second only to India in banana production and produces about 10 percent of the world's bananas.

However, our selection of bananas did not meet Mr. Ludwig's satisfaction, so he promptly sent his own private jet to Presidente Prudente to get the bananas that would best please his finicky taste buds. Jimmy and I got to ride on the jet; it was an adventure for us. Imagine sending a private plane to get a particular banana! Mr. Ludwig struck me as the very opposite of Bob Kleberg.

On a side note, Ludwig's Jari project failed miserably. Over the thirteen years the project was in his hands, he fired twenty-nine directors. The government was not happy that the project had a tax exemption. One of the two varieties of trees failed. The soil, insects, and humidity took their toll on the other variety. He couldn't keep engineers on the project because their wives were stuck in a place with no entertainment or social life. Many of the workers contracted malaria in the jungles.

Ludwig finally waved the white flag in 1981, turning the project—by this time several hundreds of millions of dollars in arrears—to a group of Brazilian businessmen.

Manchete magazine, fashioned after *Life* magazine, was a weekly news magazine published in Brazil from 1952 to 2000. It was the second most popular magazine in the country. *Manchete* (which translates to *Headline*), was splashy and colorful, and had alluring photos and covers of people such as Madonna, Princess Diana, the Beatles, Brooke Shields, Michael Jackson, Marilyn Monroe, and many others.

What does this have to do with our ranch?

Well, in 1971, the magazine did an eight-page spread on the King Ranch operations in Brazil. A journalist and a photographer came out for several days to Bartira, interviewing Dad and others and taking a

Left to right: Jimmy Emmert, Michael Emmert, Theresa Emmert, Betinha, 1971, Fazenda Bartira. Photo featured in Manchete *magazine.* Author collection.

myriad of photos of the land, the cattle, the horses, the cowboys, and unfortunately, of our family.

I say unfortunately because at the time I had braces, and I was not going to flash my metal to the vast readership. Instead, I glowered at the camera, my arms crossed, a look of defiance on my face—*No, you will* not *get me to smile*—while the photographer moved us around to various locations, placed us in assorted poses, and snapped away.

So, yes, I was in the same magazine as Marilyn Monroe, Princess Diana, and numerous other celebrities, models, and actresses. But my closed-mouth, arms-crossed pose did not exactly vault me to fame and fortune. Still—looking back, anyway—it was sort of cool to be in the magazine. And I was even on the silver screen! In those days, the movie theaters would run trailers for the magazine, because it was so popular, and the week the article came out, we got our fifteen seconds of fame. Even though I hated the picture in the trailer, I still was thrilled to see it on the big screen. My friends and I went to the movies every day that week just so we could see it. As the trailers started, they would say, "Oh! Here it comes! Watch!" The trailer was the highlight for us, not the movie—I don't even remember what movies we saw that week.

The article talked about the size of the five ranches (147,000 acres combined), the head of cattle on them (28,000), the original purchase price (8 USD per acre), and other issues related to the ranches' history.

My dad dispelled the notion of any romance involved in ranching, though the writer pegged him as the Marlboro Man for his looks and demeanor (the writer informed his readers that "This is what a *real* Texan looks like").

"It's not a romance of sitting around the campfire watching the cattle graze," Dad was quoted. "We have to grow good grass and then raise great cattle on it to produce meat as quickly as possible."

He was always focused on the quality of the grass; he cared for the land like a mother would care for her newborn. He and Bob Kleberg shared a love and passion for cultivating the land. Dad grew a variety of grasses for the pastures, but the main ones were Pangola grass, a quick-growth grass well suited to tropical climates, and Colonaio grass, another hardy grass suited to the soil and weather of Brazil.

"We do a lot of pasture renovation with legumes to increase the nitrogen level of the grasses," Dad explained to the writer. "The soil feeds the grass, the grass feeds the cattle, the cattle feed the human, and to complete the cycle, someone has to feed the soil."

That someone, of course, was him.

"A reformed pasture can handle about twice the cattle of a pasture that is not reformed," he said. "We reform about 10 percent of the land each year, plowing, discing, fertilizing, and planting peanuts, corn, sorghum, and cotton for two years before going back to pasture."

Dad also talked about how the Santa Gertrudis cattle could produce meat much quicker than the traditional Brazilian breeds, mostly zebu from India. A cross between the Santa Gertrudis and zebu resulted in a steer that could be sold at two-and-a-half years of age rather than the typical four or five years at which a full zebu could be sold. And the meat was more tender with a younger steer.

But what I remember most about the article is the picture of a thirteen-year-old girl glumly staring at the camera, obviously wishing for the stupid photo shoot she was forced to take part in to be finished. The picture was also a reminder of how Texan we looked, even though we felt so Brazilian. I guess you can take the girl out of Texas, but you can't take Texas out of the girl.

So, yes, we had many visitors over the years—a number of them pretty prestigious and well known. But perhaps the most readily known visitors whose names readers would recognize are Paul Michael Glaser and David Soul, the stars of the TV show *Starsky & Hutch*, which aired from 1975 through 1979. They came to Bartira in 1973, when I was fifteen, so this was before their time on their hit show. But they were both active as actors when they visited; David Soul had just finished starring in the show *Here Come the Brides*, and had just taken a co-starring role on the show *Owen Marshall: Counselor at Law.* Paul Michael Glaser was starring in Broadway plays and had just finished his first feature film, playing Perchik in *Fiddler on the Roof.* He was also making guest appearances on numerous shows, including *The Waltons, Kojak, The Streets of San Francisco,* and *The Rockford Files.*

Glaser and Soul knew each other before *Starsky & Hutch*—which still has a cult following—hit the screen. To this day, they call each other best friends. And that friendship was evident on their trip to Bartira. They were on vacation, had been in Rio de Janeiro, and a friend who knew about the Swift-King operations suggested that they check out the ranches. So they spent a long weekend with us, and they were about the most delightful weekend guests that we ever had. They didn't act like "movie stars"; they were down-to-earth, normal people who sported the same sharp wits and senses of humor that they would later on their show. They were fun and easy to be around, and didn't just hang out with the adults (though Dad did do a lot of touring with them around the ranch). We played "Marco Polo" with them in our swimming pool; they taught us various swimming strokes; and Paul Michael Glaser even read *Uncle Remus* books to Michael, taking over for Mom, who was reading to Michael under a gazebo in our backyard.

From just that short visit, my parents and Glaser and Soul became friends. That friendship, of course, was fueled by my mother's social nature; she was forever writing cards and letters at her colonial rolltop desk, a present from Dad that was her pride and joy (though we kids hated it because we'd experienced the rolltop banging shut on our fingers). Mom would buy UNICEF Christmas cards and send dozens of them across the globe, keeping in touch with family and friends. She had to start in early to mid-November to get them out in time. She included Glaser and Soul on her ever-expanding Christmas card list, and they sent us cards back. It was from these exchanges that the actors insisted that my parents come see them when Mom announced that they were coming to New York City, on their way to vacation in Europe.

Glaser and Soul entertained them in the city, taking them to a swanky restaurant and then bringing them back to Glaser's apartment for after-dinner drinks. My mother, of course, was thrilled with all of it, being the socialite that she was. She was in her element, while my dad was probably sitting there thinking he should be back on the ranch, working.

In many ways, my parents were a perfect match, with their extremes complementing each other, but they were far from two peas in a pod. However, I know my dad was eternally grateful that, with all of the visitors we had coming to the ranches, Mom was more than ready to take on the hosting tasks. He was happy to talk ranching and show people around, and from there he would hand things off to Mom, who played the gracious hostess for all who came to our door.

CHAPTER 12

LOOKING BACK

SPENDING THE FIRST FOURTEEN YEARS OF MY LIFE growing up on three different ranches in southeastern Brazil provided me with experiences that most US-born citizens will never have. I didn't live near a mall; I lived near a jungle. I didn't grow up watching other people's adventures on TV; I created my own adventures. I didn't watch actresses fake giving birth on television; I witnessed colony women birthing their children in their bedrooms, tended by midwives. When I got warts, I didn't go to some suburban health clinic or a pharmacy; I went to see an ancient faith healer living in a hut in a sharecropper village. I wasn't taught how to drive by a high school teacher; I learned by driving with my dad on the rough, rutted, and sometimes swamped dirt roads surrounding the ranch—and walked back to the ranch for help when I got us stuck. I didn't have a dog or a cat for a pet; I had peafowl, canaries, macaws, parrots, and Charlie the pig. I didn't ride my bike to the community pool to swim; I traipsed through a jungle to a river that had a waterfall, lots of shade, and vines and a rope to swing from and drop into the water; the river was infinitely preferable to our rather sterile pool. I didn't play with tiny, petite Barbie dolls; I played with a massive, three-foot-tall doll that had a dollhouse the size of a small hut—one in which Dad could stand up.

That last bit pretty much sums it up for me: Everything seemed larger than life in Brazil. Life had a rawer edge to it in Brazil; we were privy, growing up, to the sometimes harsh realities that life thrusts upon people who don't have the means to cushion their lives with the luxuries or conveniences that most Americans do. I'm not saying our family had it rough in Brazil; we were, actually, rather well off. In fact, I learned early on that life was easier if you were American. But we lived among the poor, we saw them living lives that were stripped of frills, that were focused on keeping food on the table.

I got to do and see things while growing up in Brazil that most American kids don't get to do and see.

I got to meet dignitaries, princesses, the mega rich, and movie stars.

I got to be in one of the best-selling magazines in Brazil.

I got to watch hundreds of cowboys expertly work with cattle and horses.

I got to go to a Candomblé ceremony and witness people in trances give messages from the dead.

I got to visit a fortuneteller who foretold my marriage to my husband, Jack.

I got to be part of the *leilões,* the cattle and horse auctions, that my parents started and that attracted upwards of a thousand people at a time.

I got to travel to and from the US many times, riding on famous state-of-the-art ocean liners.

I got to grow up on three ranches in Brazil that opened my eyes to a way of life, to a culture and a people, that were very far removed from the United States.

I got to grow up with an independent spirit, an adventurous heart, and a thirst for living life to its fullest.

And because of all of that, I got to become who I am today.

To paraphrase Robert Frost's poem, "The Road Not Taken," I took the road less traveled—one that went hither and yon through the countryside of Brazil—and that has made all the difference.

In 1981, my parents, Albert E. (Pete) Emmert and Mary Lee (Green) Emmert, returned for good to the United States. Some might see poetic justice in how it came about. Remember that my mother arranged for my dad's interview with Swift in Chicago, without his knowledge, and that interview landed them in Brazil. This time, my father did a little investigating behind the scenes and wound up with a job offer to head a ranch back in Texas before Mom knew anything was up. Dad had planted a seed in B. K. Johnson's mind when Dad and I were dropping Michael off at San Marcos Academy, a college preparatory school in San Marcos, Texas. Soon enough, B. K.—a nephew of Bob Kleberg Jr., the president of King Ranch—offered Dad a job managing the Chaparossa Ranch, which B. K. owned and which encompassed about eighty thousand acres in South Texas.

As you'll recall, my father was fine with going up to Chicago for his surprise interview with Swift back in 1958. However, my mother was *far* from fine when Dad told her he'd been offered a job in Texas. They had a rather heated discussion about Dad's subterfuge and about pulling up stakes in Brazil to return to America.

"Just come look at the ranch with me," Dad said as they faced off in the kitchen after word had gotten out.

"No," Mom said flatly.

"What do you mean, 'No'? You won't even give it a chance?"

"I cannot believe you went behind my back to get a job offer."

"I didn't go behind your back. It just happened."

"This did not 'just happen,' and you know it. You orchestrated this, every bit of it. You talked to B. K. in San Marcos, and not just about the weather."

Dad laughed scornfully. "I think you know a little about orchestration yourself. You set up my interview with Swift to get us down here in the first place without even talking to me."

"Because it was a good move! A good opportunity! You don't let this pass you by! You act on it! That's what I did."

"Fine. Well, this is a good opportunity, too. And I'm going. We've been down here for twenty-three years. That's plenty long enough."

"I don't care what you do. I'm not going."

"Fine by me. You can stay or you can go. I'm going," my dad said.

And thus, Mom entered one of her darkest moods ever, because she knew in her heart she wasn't going to be separated from dad. My dad was her rock, her everything. To be honest, it was a shock to us kids that Dad got his way, because generally when Mom wanted something badly enough, she got it—no matter who she had to run over in the process. My mother's long reign as Queen Bee in Brazil was ending—and her dethroning was not easy for her to adjust to. But adjust she did, because Mary Lee Emmert would be damned if she would let life's circumstances get the best of her.

And now, a brief rundown of many of my family members.

My dad's father, Buck, had retired, of course, by the time my parents returned to the US. He lived about three hours from the Chaparossa Ranch, but only visited my parents once. Never an overly communicative family anyway, once we moved to Brazil, the communication between my dad and Buck was largely about business: Buck handled Dad's investments back in the US. My parents still, of course, visited with Buck every time they returned to Texas.

Over the twenty-three years that my family was in Brazil, however, Buck had gotten older and ornerier, and when he died a few years after my parents moved back, my dad refused to take anything of Buck's for himself. Buck maintained his work ethic to the very end, continuing to work on saddles and taking a part-time job in a hardware store, working for his son-in-law. He'd sit in a rocker at the stove in the front of the store, telling his stories to whoever was polite enough to listen. He lived by himself until he died, and if he did not literally die with his boots on, he certainly figuratively did so.

Sadly, Dad barely outlasted his own father. Dad managed the Chaparossa Ranch from 1981 until 1992, when he was diagnosed with cancer. His "retirement" lasted six months before he died in 1993—another Emmert to work to the very end. At least he would have made Buck proud in that respect.

Even more sadly, Jimmy died in 1986 when he was a senior at Sul Ross State University in Alpine, Texas, the victim of a drunk driver. He was just three weeks away from graduating and had planned to be a park ranger. His death ripped at my heart, because he and I played and fought and laughed and pulled so many pranks together that I can't count them all. He was near and dear to my heart, and always will be.

Theresa graduated from Mom and Dad's alma mater, Texas A&M—to make Dad proud, she said—and lives in Florida, where she does booking and technical work for a resort chain that has all-inclusive resorts in the Caribbean.

Michael, my youngest sibling, lives in Houston and is a highly trained electrical worker who works on complex systems on ships, drilling rigs, and other large installations.

Theresa, Michael, and I are closer than most siblings I know. Our time in Brazil, what we shared and went through as we grew up together in a foreign country that we came to know as home, bonded us in ways that most siblings do not have the privilege to experience.

I saved my mother for last, which is the way she would expect it. (She was, after all, the Queen Bee.) We kids were not sure how she was going to respond to Dad's death; though she certainly was strong-willed and happy to share her opinion with him, more than that, she adored Dad, the love of her life. She was still young enough, with hopefully plenty left in her tank. But sometimes people just wither away when a spouse or loved one dies. So we kept in close contact with her, checking in on her multiple times a week, making sure she was doing okay, still getting out—she was, after all, the most social of butterflies.

Well, she got out, all right. In fact, to the astonishment of all, she got all the way out to the Philippines, where she was stationed after joining the Peace Corps. While there, she taught English in quite primitive conditions.

I imagine you are as stunned reading that as I am when I first heard it. Everyone—her kids, other family members, her friends—told her she was crazy. That only strengthened her resolve; no one was going to tell her what she could or couldn't do.

So she entered the Peace Corps at age sixty-three, went to the Philippines, got in with a bunch of what she called her "hippie kids," and—are you ready for this?—she actually loved it. I remember one time when Jack and I visited her in the Philippines, she asked if her friends could come over and use our hotel shower, as they didn't have running water where they were. We, of course, said sure.

Mom went on trips with, as she called them, her "young friends"; she learned how to snorkel; and she came close to getting a tattoo, "because her friends did." This just floored us. My sixty-something mother considering getting her first tattoo—"because her friends did"! Believe me, this reasoning would *not* have worked for me when I was growing up in Brazil.

Mom was in the Peace Corps for two happy years. She came back to the Corpus Christi area thin and healthy, but once she returned, her happiness faded. She had found a purpose with the Peace Corps, she had felt alive and needed and useful, but now no one needed her, and she sank into herself a bit, becoming dour and glum. Noticing this, I mentioned to her that maybe she should try dating.

"Dating? Why? I don't want sex," she said.

"I'm not talking about sex, Mom. Just go out, have fun."

"I go out and have fun, and pretty soon I'll be taking care of another sick old man." (Apparently her Peace Corps spirit did not make the trip back with her from the Philippines.)

"I'm not talking about a lifetime commitment. I'm just saying get out of the house, live a little."

Evidently my little talk with her worked, because pretty soon she called me up and said, "Guess what I'm doing next weekend?"

"What?"

"I'm going camping. With a guy."

"*Camping*? Seriously?"

"What? I was in the Peace Corps two years, you don't think I can camp for a weekend? In some fancy Airstream RV. Whatever that is."

I stifled a laugh. "So what's this guy's name?"

A pause. "I don't know. Rob, or Rod, something like that. If I like him well enough after the weekend, I'll remember his name."

After I hung up, I called Michael and told him Mom was going camping. His immediate response, after he finished laughing: "This is going to be a train wreck."

He was right. She hated the experience. She didn't have to remember the guy's name, because she would never see him again.

After returning from the Peace Corps, Mom lived another eleven years, all in Texas. She would return to Brazil every two years or so; she loved the country dearly, and I think she would have been happy to live out the rest of her days there. But those days were destined to be spent in her home state, which she lived in for twenty-six years before going on the grand adventure of her life, seven thousand miles from home.

Mom ended up in a senior living complex in Corpus Christi; but she didn't hole up in her apartment. True to her nature, she flitted about, put herself in charge of the library, made new friends to gab with and share her opinions with, and she even looked up old friends from her schoolgirl days in Sinton. She also took the helm for school reunions and get-togethers.

The complex was quite nice, and had a full-scale restaurant you could dine in, or you could cook in your own fully equipped apartment kitchen. Michael gave Mom a new cooking pan set when she entered the complex; after she passed away, we found the pans, still in their unopened box, in a cabinet. We had a good laugh over that. Mom was many things, but a cook or chef was not one of them.

She died of a stroke, which she had while sitting in a chair in her apartment one late winter evening in 2009. Apartment personnel found her in the chair the next morning; she was still alive at that point, and Michael, Theresa, and I were all called. Mom was transferred to a hospital, and I made it there before she passed, though she was in a coma and we could not speak to each other. So I just sat by her bedside and held her hand and thought back on all we had experienced together over our lifetimes, and on how she lived her life in her adopted country: Being the gracious hostess for all the social occasions and parties at the ranch—and there was always a reason to host a party. Observing her hilarious butchering of the Portuguese language while she tried to scold Brazilian clerks or waiters for falling short in some way. Buying a TV on a payment plan, sparking one of many heated discussions with Dad. Taking me shopping to Presidente Prudente and for overnight trips to São Paulo. Rescuing me from the spider monkey that had perched on my head, compliments of the Gelds. Nearly killing me when I spilled a bucket of paint on our dining room floor. Listening to her gossip with Conceicão about the goings-on in the colony. Rescuing me from my trouble after pushing a boy to the floor at my First Communion. The memories flooded back, and they worked to paint a picture of a contentious, passionate, irascible, adventurous, bullheaded, lovely, and loving woman whom I was lucky to call Mom.

She had signed Do Not Resuscitate papers; we all knew that and respected her wishes. We had certainly learned well enough by then to not cross our mother on anything so important!

So, she passed away, peacefully, her hand in mine. A few days later, we held her funeral. Her "hippie friends" in the Peace Corps sent a video of them singing many of the songs that they all sang together with my mom. All of the girls in the video were crying. The love they had for Mom was obvious. She deeply impacted lives wherever she went.

My husband, Jack, gave the eulogy for the woman who told me after she first met Jack, "He's a dirt farmer! If you marry him, you're going to be driving a combine for the rest of your life! Is that what you want?" But my mother came to love Jack, and that love was mutual.

CHAPTER 12

Well actually, I saved myself for last—sorry, Mom. Call me a chip off the old block: I need to have the last word!

Jack Schultz came to Brazil in 1974. He had recently graduated from Southern Methodist University, located in Dallas, Texas, and he spent about six weeks just traveling the country via plane, buses, and his thumb (hitchhiking was still safe enough back then), and he fell in love with Brazil. He returned to the States for graduate school, graduated in 1976, took a one-month crash course in Portuguese, and returned to Brazil, where he bought a small farm in the state of Mato Grosso do Sul (which translates to *Southern Thick Forest*). Mato Grosso is split in two, with a southern state below it—sort of like the Dakotas being split up—but before it was split, the size of the single state nearly doubled the size of Texas, and was nine times the size of Illinois. Yet, for all its massive size, it was largely undeveloped. Back then, it had one asphalted two-lane road that ran the length of the state. It was the very definition of rustic and hickish.

Well, as chance would have it, Mikey Geld was living with Jack on his farm in the southern part of the state. Mikey was managing a nearby farm but needed a place to stay, so he boarded with Jack. Mikey knew about the upcoming auction at Bartira and invited Jack to come along for something fun to do.

And that's how I first met Jack. The year was 1980.

Naturally, there were complications in the relationship we both wanted to start. My complication was named Jimmy Herbert, whom I had dated on and off for seven years (yes, the same Jimmy Herbert who drove a car while my brother Jimmy and I were hanging on for our lives on its hood). Jimmy assumed we would get married. I had a different assumption, and let Jimmy know this by tossing his engagement ring out in our yard somewhere during that auction in the spring of 1980. I don't know if he ever found the ring, and I don't care.

For his part, Jack had a girlfriend living not far from his farm. I had ditched Jimmy, and while he might have been hurt and mad, he wasn't crazy. Not so with Jack's now ex-girlfriend. She didn't politely take "No" for an answer. When Neil Sedaka wrote "Breaking Up is Hard to Do," he must have had this girl in mind. Because, one Sunday afternoon, while I was visiting Jack in his house in Dourados—he lived on the grounds of his seed-cleaning plant, in what my mother called a "shack"—a car pulled up to the house. Jack, a friend of his named Camilo, and I were sitting at the kitchen table, enjoying a cup of coffee. Camilo was the first to see the woman emerge from the car, and he immediately jumped up from the table, yelling "*Pula, pula!*", which means "jump, jump!" Camilo slammed the windows shut, but the woman responded by smashing them with her hand, in which she held a handgun.

Camilo quickly ushered me into the one bedroom in the tiny house as Jack rushed out to try to calm the girl down. Camilo and I hid in a closet as we heard the woman screaming obscenities. I gave Camilo a questioning look. "His old girlfriend," he whispered. "She doesn't like you."

I have not been liked before, but never by a person with a gun in her hand. That put a whole new spin on not being liked. I gulped and put a hand over my mouth to keep from crying out.

My screams might not have been heard, anyway, because this woman was shouting with all her might, punctuating her shouts by breaking out all the windows in the house. It was very clear that she was not only angry, she had bypassed the coffee and gone straight for the booze instead. Drunk, angry, and armed does not make for a good Sunday afternoon.

I peeked out and saw blood on Jack's shirt. My first thought was she had shot him. But I hadn't heard the gun go off, and later learned that she had cut her hand on the broken glass; it was her blood on him.

Thankfully, the ex-girlfriend's brother—apparently the designated driver for the day—came and dragged his sister out of the house, yelling at her to get a hold of herself. As soon as the coast was clear, Jack and Camilo hustled me into Jack's car, and we drove to the nearest town, which was thirty miles away, so I could get on a bus and get out of Dodge. Just as my nerves were beginning to settle, though, the car carrying Jack's ex, still being driven by her brother, pulled up alongside of us. The woman began screaming again, brandishing her gun and calling Jack and me all manner of names, none of them very nice.

"Get down!" Camilo shouted. He was driving, and Jack, from the front seat, twisted around and put his hand over my head as I ducked in the back seat. I greatly appreciated this gesture, because I wanted to live to see another day. Camilo floored it and moved ahead of Jack's ex. Later, after we arrived at the bus station, Jack checked the bus to make sure that his ex hadn't somehow beaten us there and had boarded the bus, waiting for me to get on. But it was all clear. It was a twelve-hour bus ride back to São Paulo, and I think it took about six of those hours before my heart was beating normally again.

So, you might say the beginning of our relationship had sparks flying in more ways than one. Thankfully no bullets were added to the flying sparks.

By the way, as I mentioned, Mom didn't have a terribly high opinion of Jack early on in their relationship (that changed 180 degrees over the years). The initial low opinion wasn't helped any by Mom's first impression of Jack.

That first impression came one week after the infamous "Gunfight at the Dourados Corral" incident. (Well, there was a gun involved, and the ex-girlfriend was certainly fighting.) We were all hanging out at the pool, sipping drinks; it was a hot summer day. The Gelds were visiting my parents at the time, and Carson Geld, who had more than a little zaniness in his blood—remember, he was the one responsible for Chico the monkey perching on my head when I was a toddler—had heard, probably from his son Mikey, about the ex-girlfriend fiasco. Always enjoying the opportunity to stir the hornet's nest, Carson casually said to Mom, "Hey, Mary Lee, did you hear what happened last weekend when Betinha went to visit Jack?"

My mom, who up to that point had been enjoying a grand day, sat up a bit suspiciously in her lounge chair by the pool.

We could all tell that Carson had something up his sleeve. And I knew exactly what it was.

I froze in terror, hoping against hope that he wasn't going to mention the crazy antics with the ex-girlfriend.

But then, that wouldn't be Carson's style, not to mention that incident. So I gulped, and waited, secretly trying to will Carson to say something—anything—else other than what I suspected he would say.

"Yeah, apparently she was held at gunpoint," Carson said, as nonchalantly as if he were mentioning he was thinking of going to town tomorrow.

Mom sat bolt upright in her chair, her whole body rigid. "She was *what*?" she snapped.

"I guess one of Jack's old flames showed up at his house brandishing a pistol, waving it around, shouting at Jack, demanding he bring Betinha out. Apparently, she wanted to meet Betinha," Carson said, tongue-in-cheek.

My mother, visibly shaking with anger now, turned to me, causing adrenaline to shoot through my veins and unfreeze me. "Betinha, is this—"

I didn't get to hear the word "true," because I dove into the pool as soon as my name escaped her lips. I desperately wished I had gills so I could stay under long enough for Mom to cool down, but unfortunately, I had to come up for air. As I broke the water's surface, I could hear her yelling at Jack, who stood there a bit shell-shocked. In his usual calm and low-key manner, he tried to explain to Mom what had happened.

"No, she was never held at gunpoint, Mary Lee, nothing like that, I can assure you," Jack said, casting a quick and rather unthankful eye

Carson's way. Carson appeared not to notice, and just went on sipping his drink.

Seeing my head above water, Mom shouted at me, "Were you held at gunpoint?"

"No! Didn't you just hear Jack say I wasn't?"

"Yes, but I don't know who or what to believe." She gave Jack a scathing look.

"Well, believe Jack! And me! And it's not his fault his ex-girlfriend is nuts, is it?"

"So what exactly did happen, then?" Mom asked.

Jack and I tag-teamed on a sanitized version of the story, skipping over the more lurid details.

"Well, what's he doing with a girl like that in the first place, anyway?" Mom asked when we were finished.

I groaned. "The bottom line is, I'm fine, no one was hurt, and that girl is out of the picture. So just forget it. Okay?"

Mom rolled her eyes as she got up from her chair to go inside the house. "I hope you know what you're getting yourself into," she muttered as she walked away.

Once she was gone, I gave Carson the dirtiest look I could. "Thanks a lot, Carson."

"No problem," he replied. He looked quite satisfied, to be honest. Certainly he was the only one to enjoy the exchange.

Once Jack's ex was out of the picture (and no, we didn't put a hit out on her; she just disappeared to torment someone else), things calmed down. We got married in 1981, he sold his farm in Brazil, and we moved to Effingham, Illinois. It's where we still live—and Jack did not turn out to be a dirt farmer. Since the mid 1980s, he has been CEO of Agracel, Inc., an industrial developer of facilities for manufacturing and high-tech entities in small to midsized communities; he is a book author; he has served on various boards of trustees and directors; he is past

Elizabeth (Betinha) Schultz and husband Jack Schultz.
Author collection.

president of the Illinois State Universities Retirement System; and he also served as chairman of the board of Midland States Bank for many years, helping to take it public on NASDAQ in 2016. Oh, and he earned an MBA from Harvard.

So no, Mom, I didn't marry a dirt farmer; I married the love of my life, a love that first took hold on a Swift-King ranch down in Brazil, and that has deepened and blossomed in the American Midwest. Meeting Jack was the best thing that ever happened to me, just like meeting Mom was the best thing to ever happen to Dad—and vice versa.

Jack and I return frequently to Brazil. The country holds special meaning for us both. For me, it is where I grew up, where I learned, as my mother once said, that "Life is like bull wrangling."

Once that bull runs out of the chute, she told me, "you have to grab your opportunity at the exact right moment. You can't hesitate or doubt yourself. You just jump on the damn bull and wrangle it."

That's how Mary Lee Emmert lived her life. And that's how she taught me to live mine, too.